Managing an Estate Without Paper Records

Ronald J. Leach

Published by AfterMath, 2024.

While every precaution has been taken in the preparation of this book, the publisher assumes no responsibility for errors or omissions, or for damages resulting from the use of the information contained herein.

MANAGING AN ESTATE WITHOUT PAPER RECORDS

First edition. April 22, 2024.

ISBN: 979-8224601660

Written by Ronald J. Leach.

Also by Ronald J. Leach

Software Reuse: Methods, Models, Costs, Second Edition
Why 2K?
Where Have All The Templars Gone?
User Guide to Microfilm and Microfiche
The 101 Most Important UNIX and Linux Commands
Baltimore Blue and Freddie Gray
Digitizing Microfilm and Microfiche
Managing an Estate Without Paper Records

Table of Contents

To David

Introduction

This practical book is intended for anyone who has recently been bereaved and believes that he or she will assume responsibility for managing an estate with a large digital legacy. Unfortunately, one of the lingering effects of the covid-19 epidemic was the work-from-home movement and resulting changes in staffing in government and financial institutions that affect estates. Many additional difficulties have arisen because changing work environments have been coupled with many efforts to change administrative processes to ones that are primarily online. Learning how to navigate these complexities is especially relevant in the primary focus of this book — how to create and manage a n estate if these are few or no actual paper records.

The discussion here is based on my own experiences when my son died of the Covid-19 virus during the height of that epidemic. I believed that the estate had significant value at the time of death and required reestablishing multiple revenue streams for potential future digital business earnings.

I knew nothing about the banks that he used or any brokerage or investment account that he may have had. There were no paper records at all, and this lack caused enormous problems when it came to managing his estate.

The practical advice given here is especially relevant in the changed world in which most financial dealings are best done remotely using phones and computers. In fact, with long-term changes in many financial industries, performing many of the duties of an estate administrator can be done only remotely because of reduced office staffs in many financial and government offices. There simply isn't much of a paper trail in many cases, and there may not even be a paper trail at all. Even if there is a paper trail, you probably can't do much of the estate's business via snail mail or in person. Physical property, including a house or its contents, perhaps, but not much of the deceased's digital life.

Here's why. You'll recall that enormous societal changes occurred during that epidemic. Many schools went to remote learning, either partially or totally. The effects of that seismic change which no one in the education field had planned for, are showing up now in the form of lower skill levels of students. With many school age children now at home during the day, many parents did not go to their normal workplace, even if their workplace was open. Some workers in some types of businesses were able to, and often required to, work from home. The demand for telemedicine services greatly increased.

For a time, the US Post Office had great difficulty providing reliable mail service, due to staffing changes, reorganization, and many other issues. Wearing masks all day was extremely tiring, especially for workers who needed to wear them all day. Mail delivery still seems very slow.

Since many workers who had gone to workplaces previously were now working at home, companies that once ran restaurants and hotels now had few, if any, customers. Office buildings were essentially vacant. Many businesses closed.

Other companies recognized the opportunity to go digital. Banks that had served a large number of office workers who had been walk-in customers during the day closed many of their branches in some areas. Brokerages did the same. Government services often were provided by workers who could do their jobs remotely from home could now do so, provided that they had reliable access to necessary data and a good internet connection. The same trend of moving to remote service remains true for many jobs in the private sector, especially those in the financial industry.

The only guidance I had in handling my son's estate was a remembered conversation when his mother and I asked what he wanted done with his online businesses in case of unexpected death and he said that everything will go to his minor daughter. He was divorced and his ex-wife had remarried since. I knew it was my responsibility to make sure his wishes were carried out. Fortunately, my ex-daughter-in-law and I were on very good terms so that she was able to take both the initial and the yearly distributions that I would make from the estate and put them to good use in my granddaughter's education and for other needs..

I knew that my son had been both an author of ebooks and also an ebook publisher. I knew he had been to China and to several international book fairs where he had arranged with both authors and publishers to publish their books. I did not know any details about his specific arrangements with any publishers.

This book describes my journey to make this financial analysis and reconstruction of businesses happen. It is presented in roughly the order of what I had done and the many things that had to be done, with some differences when hindsight makes it clear that I should have done some things differently. (There is one exception to this. One of the first steps in managing any deceased person's estate is obtaining an official death certificate. I have placed the discussion of that issue at the end of the narrative, because it was an extremely complicated process due to Covid and still is extremely painful for anyone to read.)

There were successes and failures. One of the most helpful accomplishments was being able to see all the files on his two computers, even without knowing the passwords. A custodial estate account was set up for the benefit of my minor granddaughter. The companies that our son had been receiving payments from were contacted and revenue streams were sent to the appropriate custodial account. Bank accounts, stockbrokerage accounts, IRAs, Treasury bills, and the like were found and sent to the right places. Most, but not all, of the business income earned after his death, was able to be transferred to the custodial account for his daughter. Other moneys, including a larger than expected refund from an insurance company were found using a state website devoted to handling unclaimed money deposited into the estate account.

The failures were all caused by the same problem —the restrictive privacy policies of most tech companies, including many telecom companies. Due to recent policy changes, there are now ways to get at least some access to a deceased person's online data. We discuss such methods in a chapter near the end of this book as well as ways that readers of this book can arrange for access to their affairs in the event of an untimely death..

As with most things in life, solving a complicated problem required some help. My wife, daughter, son-in-law, and ex-daughter-in-law were all extremely helpful. We used the offices of the same attorney who had created our will to explain the processes involved, create the estate, and handle some of the correspondence. She and her staff solved many problems. There were many helpful conversations with bereavement sections of multiple banks and companies. I also had help from several state and government offices. Some personnel at tech companies provided assistance, even though they could not provide access to accounts due to privacy policies.

About me: I was retired, so had the time to navigate phone trees to seek out essential helpful personnel at multiple organizations.

The last twenty-five years of my career were spent as a Professor of Computer Science, with nine of those years as a department Chair. So, even though I have been retired since 2010, I know a lot about computers. I had even written a book on data recovery.

This level of computer knowledge shouldn't scare you, however. There are only two paragraphs in this entire book that describe anything that a person who uses the Internet, email, and how to create a file and write a message using something like *Microsoft Word* or create an *Excel* spreadsheet would not be able to do. These two paragraphs are written at the level of a brief article or technical advice column that might appear in a newspaper or online news feed.

I learned a lot of things during the process of recreating this estate and have included information on all of them here. I hope this book helps you deal with such an unpleasant task. Be sure to use the contact information and website information given in the References chapter.

This book is available in both electronic and print formats.

First Steps

My wife and I were among the first people to learn of our son's death during the Covid-19 epidemic. We were notified that he had died when two officers of the Baltimore City Police Department came to our house late one night and told us. The officers had been asked to investigate by neighbors because there was a box of Chewy dog food that had been left on the steps for several days. The officers were highly professional and tried to console us appropriately. They provided us with a business card that had contact information for the lead officer, the Chief Medical Examiner, and for a company that specialized in doing Covid-19 bioremediation.

We notified our daughter about her brother's death that night. The next day we contacted our ex-daughter-in-law about the death and told her that, with her permission, we would handle things for a while. She would handle the possibility of telling her daughter. I was the only one who would be allowed to have any access to our deceased son's house until after I had met with the bioremediation company technician, the bioremediation was completed, and the house was considered to be safe.

Early the next morning, we contacted the bioremediation company and we arranged for a team that they sent over to our son's house a few hours later. Our always helpful son-in-law came over to help, providing some sealable plastic boxes that he thought I would need.

The lead bioremediation technician took us through the process and I signed some paperwork. There was homeowners insurance on the contents of the house and we were told what to say when I talked to the insurance company. The technician had made a rough estimate of the interior dimensions of the corner Baltimore City townhouse. Then the technician donned a hazmat suit and went inside to do an initial inventory. The bioremediation protocols required discarding the hazmat suit and putting on a new one every two hours.

I let the bioremediation technician into the house and awaited his report. As my son-in-law and I waited outside, many of my son's friends and neighbors came by and told us lovely stories of their interactions. I gave the unopened carton of Chewy dog food that had been left on the front steps to a friendly dog owner.

The Contents of The House

The bioremediation technicians' initial assessment was that there were two laptop computers and connecting cables, a cell phone on a Cricket Wireless plan, and a tablet (not an *iPad* or a Microsoft *Surface*). There was also a wallet and a set of keys. There were no paper records of any sort, so everything in the way of financial information that I had was in the wallet or electronics. The bioremediation company technician said that this was the smallest amount of paper records he had ever seen.

I decided that all of these items would undergo special sterilizing treatment bioremediation and be searched later for relevant information after there was no danger of contamination. When the technician brought these items outside, he sprayed them with some special liquid. He then took off his hazmat mask and discarded it. I took that as being a sign that he, the expert, felt it was safe to have the items in my possession. Therefore, I asked the bioremediation technicians to place them in one of the sealable plastic boxes my son-in-law had brought and enclosed it in an ultra-heavy sealable trash bag. I would leave everything sealed for four days, which was the commonly agreed upon time that the virus could survive without a host.

There were also two televisions, a cable box, soft goods, furniture, built-in appliances, a few countertop appliances, utensils, food, and clothing, and draperies present in the house. All obvious hideaways were searched at this time. (I did a more thorough search after the house was considered safe enough for me to enter. Nothing relevant was found.) This was the totality of physical goods in the house. It was decided that everything in this category would undergo bioremediation but that it would all be discarded for safety reasons except for the built-in appliances, which would be sprayed thoroughly with the biohazard remediation material.

(Of course, a different decision would have been made if there was anything of value left in the house. When cleaning out the Florida condominium of my aunt after her death in Baltimore, I found one of her neighbors, a self-acclaimed friend going through her belongings. I demanded the key and changed the lock. There was nothing to steal in the case of this house.)

Only the cable box and the built-in appliances were to be left inside the house.

The complete bioremediation process took four days, so it would probably have been safe to open the sealed plastic boxes at that time. Just to be sure, I waited a few more days before I did anything with the computers.

Fortunately, the bioremediation technician had provided contact information for a man with a truck who would haul away all the remaining contents of the house. The man did an excellent job, taking two trips to remove everything that needed to be moved. He said he could do some small repair jobs and I parceled them out over a period of time, adding more responsibilities as I saw what he was able to do. After a number of jobs were completed, I gave him a key rather than trying to connect with him on a daily basis. This was easier, because meeting him at a time when nearby parking was available was not always convenient. (As stated before, the only things worth stealing were the old built-in appliances, which we replaced when we put the house up for sale.)

Notifying Relevant Parties

My wife and I held title to the house for tax purposes, and we decided to sell it instead of trying to rent it. Since winter was coming, we were responsible for utilities, so we left the heat, electric, and water on. The Baltimore Gas and Electric Company and the City of Baltimore would have all of their regular bills paid and the last month's shares would be prorated at the time of sale. These bills did not need to have the responsible party changed.

Our daughter arranged for cancellation with the company that provided health insurance.

I contacted the cable provider and asked if they wanted the cable box back. They said no, perhaps thinking of the risks of possible exposure to the virus, so all that was needed to do was to pay the final bill.

We notified our son's friends that we knew about. As stated before, while waiting outside his house for the technician, I was approached by several of his local friends and neighbors who offered condolences and told us wonderful stories. I knew he was a karaoke fan, but did not know that he often ran karaoke nights for several local establishments.

I cancelled the monthly subscription that had been arranged to have dog food from chewy.com[1] delivered. The neighbors thought this was the only regular delivery that came to the house.

There was nothing more that we could do, because of a delay in obtaining the death Certificate from the Medical Examiner. As stated previously, this delay is described in a separate chapter of this book. Unfortunately, this delay caused problems getting access to financial assets and records.

I had difficulty providing an obituary notice to the greatly understaffed *Baltimore Sun* Newspaper. Normally, they would run the obituary in both the *Baltimore Sun* and the *Howard County Sun* (our son was born and raised in Columbia, in nearby Howard County, Maryland). I couldn't get the obituary submitted online - and me, a computer scientist! I couldn't drop it off at the paper's editorial offices, because they weren't admitting visitors. Mail delivery was not an option because the Post Office had so many organization and other problems at that time. Finally, I was able to find the contact information for the

---

1.   http://chewy.com

person who wrote most of the paid obituaries, called him up, told him what I wanted, and he sent a staff member down to the newspaper's front door to take the obituary that I provided on a USB flash drive along with a check.

Talk to a Lawyer!

Fortunately, my wife and I had a longstanding relationship with the aforementioned competent law firm. I had first heard the founder speak at one of those typical information sessions about wills and trusts that various investment companies held at a local hotel and had contacted him years ago while my wife and I were still working. We had set up an appointment to make up wills then and it was certainly appropriate to have a new will drawn up. We invited our daughter to come to the new meeting, since she would now be the exclusive executor, with advice provided if necessary from an out-of-town banker relative. A long-term employee of the law firm had obtained her law degree and had become a full partner, and she and her paralegal staff handled the entire complex situation we had.

I had had experience with estates previously. I had been the administrator of my mother's estate, which was relatively simple. There was a Social Security benefit for funeral expenses and her house and her savings account were jointly owned by me. I had advice from our previous long-term lawyer about death certificates and the like. I also was the executor for an aunt who had been a Florida resident but had died in Maryland. Everything she had was owned jointly with me and I used the names of original co-owners of two savings accounts that had been set up in Florida as a guide to her wishes when I dispersed checks to them. (The recipients of these unexpected checks were grateful.)

One thing I had learned from my previous experience with the estates of relatives who died in Maryland was that nearly all things with joint ownership automatically passed on to the surviving owner without going through the estate. Be sure to check on the laws in your state. Also, keep in mind that federal laws may differ from state laws.

While we were sitting there in our lawyer's office it was appropriate to ask for other legal advice in this complicated legal situation. A search of legal records by the attorney showed what I had suspected — there was no will. The legal term for this situation is "dying intestate."

Of greater concern was that the most obvious person to be a recipient of the estate was unable to do so legally, because she was a minor. As noted before, my wife and I still had a good relationship with my ex-daughter-in-law and she had indicated that she was willing to give me permission to manage the estate as the Estate Administrator. The lawyer drew up the paperwork to allow me to become the Estate Administrator.

Of course, nothing could be done until a Death Certificate could be issued. More about _that_ experience in the chapter entitled "Getting The Death Certificate."

The attorneys said that they had someone they could recommend at that time who was an expert in getting access to computers. I passed on that opportunity then, but reserved the ability to call on those services at a later time if I was unable to get access myself. (Although I, as a former Computer Science Chair, had employed several people who could do that, I decided to not ask any of them for help, or even discuss this issue, because it seemed an unethical action to take with any former employee or colleague even if I paid for their service.) As you will see, getting access turned out to be very easy and I am sure that readers of this book will be able to to get access as long as the data on any relevant computers weren't encrypted.

There was an unforeseen advantage to working with these attorneys. They had an excellent paralegal who handled some negotiations with three organizations that had money that either had been held for my son or was considered as part of a future revenue stream. Two of these organizations were international.

Create an Estate

I was asked about the amount of money and other assets that would be in my son's estate and I gave my best answer. I was unaware of any substantial cash on hand, and did not know anything specific about stocks, bonds, mutual funds, or real estate that he owned. I knew that he had had serious business reversals several years ago and had made some new business ventures, but I knew almost nothing abut them. He seemed to have had serious cash flow problems at times. (We later learned that most of his funds were kept in online investments accounts in stocks and in treasuries.)

Not being sure of my rights and responsibilities in this matter, I decided to not look through the contents of my son's wallet, and not even think about examining his computer. I wanted to wait until I received proper authority to be the administrator of the estate.

Besides, as indicated previously, I wanted to wait at least four more days as was indicated previously before looking at anything inside that sturdy plastic box to make sure that there was no live Covid-19 virus.

The attorney had some very good advice: a small estate is easier to deal with than a large one because it avoids probate. The point was obvious. Why should you have to deal with the hassle and expense of going through probate if you don't have to so so? I saw my responsibility as obtaining as much money for the benefit of my minor granddaughter as possible, and not expend any unnecessary funds on legal fees.

In the state of Maryland, a small estate is one that is valued at under $50,000. I am not sure what the limit is in other states. Since this might be a legal question for you, I strongly recommend that you search this matter and get legal advice if necessary.

Did my son's estate qualify as a small estate? I had no record of any ownership of stocks, bonds, mutual funds, or real estate. It was not clear that his suspected publishing arrangements would continue to exist and that any future royalties would be paid. (I suspected that there might be some royalties that might be payable to the estate, but any such royalties could not be expected to be estimated accurately at this time.)

There was a wallet, but I had decided not to examine it before the estate was formally created and I became its official Administrator. Thus, I assumed the estate was a "small estate" because there were few known assets.

(I knew that there my deceased son owned no real estate, because the house that he and his wife had jointly owned had become the sole property of my ex-daughter-in-law in the divorce. Of course, you should check for the existence of any real estate the deceased person owned if you become the administrator of an estate.)

Become the Estate Administrator

I finally received the official Death Certificates from the Medical Examiner's Office. This information, coupled together with whatever legal magic our lawyer practiced, allowed the estate to be set up and me to become the Estate Administrator and Personal Representative for a Small Estate. In Maryland there are two types of relevant forms: the Creation of Small Estate and the Letter of Administration. Your state might differ.

Apparently, the state of Maryland's primary concern at this point in the life of an estate is making sure that the funeral home or funeral society gets paid for any services that were performed as part of a funeral, burial, or cremation. Feeling that all moneys in the estate should go to our granddaughter and not to overhead, we had already paid the funeral home out of our own personal funds.

At the second meeting with our attorney, my wife and I were told that we could have been repaid out of the estate, because it was a legitimate estate responsibility. I suspect we would have done so if there had been multiple people with potential claims to the estate. Instead, as we mentioned, we paid that bill ourselves, wishing to leave more for our granddaughter.

The issue of setting up an estate account is sufficiently complicated, and it is where I made my first mistake while managing the estate. (I carelessly used the wrong name of the estate on a tax form, using the name of the bank account set up for the estate instead of the name on the EIN form from the IRS. This caused some tax ramifications in the first year of the estate's existence. See the chapter on Banking for more information.)

You will certainly need to keep accurate records, both in digital and paper form. I suggest the following as a minimum.

- On your computer, create a new folder to keep all documents. Have digital copies of all legal documents in this folder.

- Create a new email address for use with any estate business. I find this much better than using a separate "smart folder" in an existing email account. Make sure that there are no restrictions that are likely to be imposed as to message size, because a digital email account for an estate might generate a lot of digital files.

• Use a collection of cardboard folders to keep different types of paper records in. As a minimum, keep a folder for all copies of administration forms, one for all tax records, one for all bank statements, one for each other type of financial institution you deal with. Keep all these folders in the same place.

• Make sure you understand any business, especially ones that is solely digital, in order to obtain any unexpected income.

• Pay all federal and state taxes at the appropriate time. Normally, the estate would have to pay taxes yearly.

• Make disbursements to beneficiaries, either ones actually mentioned in a will, or one who is presumed, because of a relationship, as in the case of a minor child and the deceased dying intestate, at the appropriate time. Try to make sure that the amount disbursed in each year is greater than the amount of any income paid to the estate in that year, if possible, in order to minimize the amount of taxable income. As much as possible, plan to receive business income in the same or subsequent years, so as to minimize taxes.

• Think about succession of the business, and have a method to show year-by-year profits and estate tax forms to be able to show to any potential buyer in case the business is sold.

• Keep a record of all conversations with any entities, whether financial or personal. Be sure to keep all contact information.

Think Like the Deceased Person

The title of this chapter may seem like an odd thing to consider. However, certain events in my son's life clearly had an effect on his thinking about financial matters, and that information gained from my understanding of these events guided my search for his assets. As you will see, those events inform the discussion in this chapter.

As many parents do, we had set up bank accounts for our children. Since we believed in supporting local institutions, we chose to set up these accounts at a savings and loan association branch located in a small nearby shopping center. The association was named Old Court Savings and Loan, and it paid a high rate of interest on savings accounts. The deposits there were insured by the state-sponsored Maryland Savings Share Insurance Corporation (MSSIC) so we thought they were safe

They were not! Old Court could pay high interest rates because it made risky loans, a fact we were unaware of when we opened these accounts. In 1985, there were rumors of insolvency. We were eating breakfast while reading the Saturday issue of *The Washington Post* and we read an article that suggested that Old Court might fail. We rushed the kids to get dressed and find their passbooks (remember those?) after which we would walk over as a group to take out our funds. Old Court was only open until noon on Saturdays.

Unfortunately, our youngest son could not locate his passbook so the rest of us went there without him. The Old Court branch office was packed and the head teller kept telling us that everything was alright, that everyone should relax and go home. No one did. The other tellers were told not to close accounts. Finally, after the crowd of customers got larger and louder, the many customers were told that if we lined up quietly, we could close our accounts. Everyone there did so, getting all their funds back.

Not so our youngest son. Old Court was soon closed, and there were rumors that the MSSIC was not fully funded in the same way as were accounts insured by the FDIC that had been created during the Depression to reassure bank customers of the safety of their money. We soon found out that the rumors were correct.

The Governor of Maryland issued an executive order limiting withdrawals to $1,000 per month from any savings and loan association in Maryland, and there were two special sessions of the state legislature to replace the MSSIC by the newly established Maryland Deposit Insurance Fund (MDIF). Our youngest got his funds after waiting six months.

I suspect that, from my deceased son's perspective, the situation was far too much like the bank failures during the Depression, something that my parents had lived through but had often described to me, my wife, and our children. He never really trusted banks, and would have preferred digital transactions once the Internet could be used for electric banking

These experiences help explain why he had two local accounts, at banks that I will call bank #1 and bank #2. Separating the income streams of his businesses into two categories protects against bank failures, and against any legal action against one of the royalty paying companies spilling over to cut off bank access.

Bank #1 was used for income that was generated from international companies: the Italian company StreetLib.com[1] with an office in New York that we have already mentioned, and immateriel.fr[2], which is a French company that had no offices in the United States. The French company was the source of the mysterious royalty income that was paid into our son's bank account using PayPal. We'll discuss immateriel.fr[3] later. Bank #2 received income directly from Apple and Kobo for sales of ebooks. We will discuss my experiences with bank #1 and bank #2 in the chapter on banking.

The last job my son had before starting his entrepreneurial efforts was as a member of the technical support staff of a branch of major publisher that produced investment reports and analyses. He learned a lot about the stock market and investments, and near the end of his time as an employee, he seemed to believe that he could detect trending companies and industries in certain areas, and that he could do so as well as most of his colleagues who were paid to be stock analysts. This was at a time before the rise of so-called

---

1.   http://StreetLib.com

2.   http://immateriel.fr

3.   http://immateriel.fr

"quants," who were experts in evaluating micro-trends, and also before the rise of super-fast connections between brokerage firms that allowed organizations intending to make a trade to either buy sell a large number of stocks to probe the market with small trades to discern patterns of the stock prices going up or down tiny amounts before making any large transaction.

He learned how to read available information about company balance sheets and was an astute investor. We always made money following his stock tips. At times he did exceptionally well. As we learned, in the process of researching his estate, all his investments were made online.

He also learned about constant cyber attacks against many companies and how to defend against most of them. He felt comfortable with designing his own website and protecting it. He also tried to be as anonymous as possible, using a made-up name for use in his business and several company names. He also changed email addresses often, always moving in the direction of greater privacy and encryption.

He had moved several times after the end of his marriage and thus saw no value in keeping paper records, because of the difficulty of making sure that his mail was forwarded properly.

So how did this information affect my search for his assets? Here are the assumptions that I had made before beginning a search for his assets.

- There were no additional bank accounts other than the ones associated with the bank cards in his wallet.

- He was extremely knowledgeable about money and related financial matters.

- Any brokerage account would be online only.

- He would not use a brokerage firm associated with a bank.

- He would not invest in any mutual fund other than perhaps an index fund, because he preferred to make his own decisions about buying or selling stocks.

• He would not have physical records of any stock. In particular, he would not have physical stock certificates.

• He would change email addresses frequently, always moving in the direction of greater security and privacy, and with greater encryption.

• He often used different company names, believing that maximum separation was a good idea.

• His professional life was essentially digital.

• He was capable of organizing his business and protecting it against hackers.

Armed with this knowledge, I was ready to begin my search for his assets in a systematic way. This required me to gain access to his computer files and to start searching for financial assets. I did the two almost simultaneously because every piece of information I could find would help in the discovery process.

I had several constraints. Because I believed that the intended beneficiary of the estate was a minor child, I was unaware of any financial assets. (I never thought that information about the marital assets of my son and his wife were any of my business. I knew that anything in both their names would fall directly to my ex-daughter-in-law after the no-fault divorce, and not go to the estate. It was my responsibility to search for assets, and to make sure assets went directly to her if they were, in fact, joint assets, and that any other assets would go to the estate.)

Records and Forms

As the executor and Administrator of an estate, you will need to keep accurate records for both the time before and after his or her death. Just think about what happens if someone makes a claim against the estate, or, even worse, against you as the Administrator. Even if no actual legal claim is made, there may be hard feelings and a lack of trust about the timing and amount of distributions of the estate. If you are an Administrator, part of your job is to keep accurate records, and another part is to handle the financials properly.

We will separate the two types of things we consider in this chapter by when they occurred: those that existed before the time of death and after, once the estate is created. We note that if a person is unable to manage their affairs for any period even before their death, and you have taken over management of the estate, records will need to be kept.

Records to Keep

The list below provides a general scheme for the records you will try to locate and keep, even if many of the issues do not apply, as is this case of a death occurring during the height of the Covid-19 virus epidemic and leaving no paper records or passwords. We do not claim that this list will be complete in every foreseeable circumstance. (As was indicated before, there were no written records found.)

- List of always critical vital records. This includes birth, marriage, and divorce records. These will be duplicated elsewhere, but may be hard to access.

- Medical records.

- Medical power of attorney and and advanced directives.

- List of possible beneficiaries.

- Wills, if any.

- List of other valued assets and any plans for their dispersal if not explicitly stated as a codicil in a will.

- Lists of properties owned or rented. Remember that leases have values.

- All relevant estate creation papers.

- Recent bank records, going back at least one year.

- Old tax returns.

- All computers and computer files.

- All passwords to all accounts, including cloud storage accounts.

- All valuable photos. (The term "valuable" includes any family heirlooms, regardless of any financial value.)

- List of assets, in either physical or digital format.

- List of recurring liabilities.

- List of non-recurring liabilities.

- List of all planned or actual charitable distributions.

- SSN and/or EIN.

- New bank account for estate.

- Plan for dispersal of assets.

- A journal or log of activities.

- List of bank interactions.

- List of brokerage interactions.

- Searches for unclaimed funds.

- Papers for business or businesses.

You should keep all these records as long as you reasonably can. Physical items that you do not wish to keep should be kept, even in storage if necessary, until time of probate if there is a will to be probated, and decisions about disbursements of assets will need to have been made. They may be necessary if any of your actions as an estate administrator are questioned.

Forms to Fill Out

You will have to fill out many forms as an Administrator of an estate. These records should be kept during the time that the estate exists, and some time afterwards, in order to protect you and/or your own heirs against possible legal action. Some of these are listed below.

- EIN for the estate.

- W-9 for the estate

- Complete set of bank statements for the duration of the estate account. This will include records of all monies dispersed.

- Complete set of statements from brokerages for the duration of the estate account.

- Change of address forms, if necessary.

- Federal estate tax forms (initial, then yearly.)

- State estate tax forms (initial, then yearly).

- Succession plans for the business.

These records should be made available to you in a convenient location and kept until at least five years after the estate is closed. (The five-year period may be different in other states. Also, federal rules may differ from state rules. See your attorney for more information.)

Social Security

There are several kinds of interactions that will probably have to occur between you (as estate administrator) and the Social Security Administration.

- The Social Security Administration will have to be notified of the death of the decedent. The funeral home may do this if they have the deceased's Social Security Number. You can contact Social Security directly. See ssa.gov[1].

- There is a death benefit, currently in the amount of $265.

- A minor child who has had a parent die will be able to receive benefits until he or she reaches the age of 18. This benefit will have to be applied for. (I informed my ex-daughter-in-law about this benefit and she applied for it directly in her daughter's behalf.)

- A minor child who has had a parent die and who is considered disabled generally will be able to receive additional benefits until he or she reaches the age of 18. This disability benefit will have to be applied for. (This type of benefit did not apply in this particular case.)

---

1. http://ssa.gov

Setting Up The Estate Account.

It was now time to examine the wallet. I no longer feared catching the Covid-19 virus from my son's possessions after they had been untouched such a long period in a quarantine. What did I find?

- Nationally recognized credit cards for two different accounts from the same credit card provider. One of these cards had expired.

- ATM cards (bank debit cards) for three banks, one of which seemed to be based primarily in Puerto Rico and the other two were national banks that had many branches in Maryland. These cards could also serve as credit cards, although I later found that they had never been used for that purpose,

- Various identification cards.

- A driver's license issued in the state of Maryland.

- A Social Security card. (We already had his Social Security Number, which had been issued at his birth.)

- A Passport Card used for international travel. (He had used this on a trip that he and I took to Egypt together the year before.)

- Various other items not relevant to the issue of creating an estate.

I now had something to work with. I took out a pad of paper and started to keep a paper record of what I had found and how I had done it.

I called the credit card company first. Since I had not seen any paper records, and had been informed by the bioremediation technician that he saw no paper records, I assumed that he received his bills online. Since I had not yet decided how to proceed in getting access to his computers, making the call was the right decision.

On the call to the 800 number listed on a credit card, I got through the extensive phone option tree, finally getting a human providing customer service for bereaved persons. I identified myself and my relationship to the cardholder as the personal representative of the estate, gave the credit card number for the card that had <u>not</u> expired, and my son's Social Security number. Then I waited for the credit card company's representative to lookup the details of the account and, presumably, the relevant state laws and policies. After a few minutes, I found that the card had an outstanding balance due. The good news was that the estate was not responsible for any outstanding balance

I repeated the same process for the credit card that <u>had</u> expired and received the same answer from the credit card company: the estate was not responsible for any outstanding balance. I thanked the customer service representative for the help and disconnected.

Unfortunately, I was so happy about having the estate debts forgiven by the credit card company that I forgot to ask for a set of recent statements. Such statements would have shown recent transactions to website hosting companies, and the like. I only realized my mistake when I started writing this book and discovered what I had done in haste.

Tip: Be sure to get a year's worth of credit card statements.

Banking

There are so many issues with regards to banking that we will devote a section of this chapter to each of them. Before we start, let's review what we said previously about the availability of banking, credit unions, and other financial services in the introduction.

"Banks that had served a large number of office workers who had been walk-in customers during the day closed many of their branches in some areas. Brokerages did the same. Government services often were provided by workers who could do their jobs remotely from home could now do so, provided that they had reliable access to necessary data."

Keep this in mind because it confirms why some of the decisions made sense to me at the time they were made, but may seem like being poor ideas in hindsight.

There is one more thing to mention before we discuss banking issues in detail. Since my son's business was a sole proprietorship, the business was technically closed after his death and the stream of royalty payments would be stopped from the publishers to his account. These revenue streams would have to be restarted, with new accounts and tax IDs created.

Clearly, getting a bank account for the estate was the next step. But where? I needed information.

The next useful information came the two US-based banks that I found ATM cards for. One was a bank that had a branch right around the corner from my son's house. And that branch was still open! Unlike many large national banks, this bank did not close any of its branches in Baltimore City during the height of the virus. I called for an appointment with a knowledgeable employee and was able to get one the next day. (I had been to that same branch a few days before, explaining the situation and asking what I needed to bring with me. The bank officer and all the other personnel I dealt with were very helpful.) I'll often refer to this bank as bank #1.

During my appointment, I was able to get paper records for the previous eighteen months worth of bank statements on the existing account. I could have gotten records farther back in time for a fairly reasonable fee, but decided not to do this since I saw little value in doing so. I could see where money was coming from, and could verify that there were no recurring charges that were paid directly from that bank account. There was no affiliated brokerage account, as I had expected.

There were two primary income streams that were paid monthly. One of them was with a company that I had heard of but did not really know. I recalled my son forwarding to me an email from an Italian company named StreetLib, saying "I'm back in the print business." So I now had someone to contact to make sure that some income from that source would be directed into the proper account. The original account had to be closed and a new account opened because of laws that are probably common to each state.

Tip: See if your state allows multiple Administrators or Personal Representatives of a Small Estate.

There was a second source of income from a source that I did recognize — PayPal. However, I did not know at the time what company had been sending payments via PayPal. Fortunately, I did find out that information a few months later. This was the limit of how far I could go without a tax ID (EIN). (See below.)

I would have liked to have had this new estate account set up jointly with my former daughter-in-law, but this was not possible. Perhaps, the estate could have been set up as having two co-executors or personal representatives. I don't know if that would have been possible, because it would have been difficult for her to take any actions in obtaining what I believed was one of the estate's main assets — the royalties obtained from future income streams.

The first step in setting up an estate account is for the estate to set up a tax ID, also known as a EIN (Employer Identification Number). You can do this yourself, but it is probably better to get the number at the same time as the creation of the new estate bank account. The bank can do this directly, and the issuing of the number is often immediate.

Unfortunately, "often" does not mean "always." The estate account at the bank was created (pending the allocation of an EIN) in the later part of

December in 2020. The IRS office that issues EINs was closed, with an automated message that it would reopen January 4, 2021. In fact, the ability of the IRS to create an EIN was not available until January 7, 2021.

Tip: Get an EIN before you do anything financial.

The actual EIN was sent as an email to both the bank where it was set up and to me as the estate administrator at the email address I provided. (I had set up an email address for the estate previously.) My name and the abbreviation ADM appeared in the net line of the email message. Don't lose it!

The number came in the format below:

FirstName MiddleName LastName Estate

The name of the bank account that I had created earlier that day had a similar name:

Estate of *FirstName MiddleName LastName*

Unfortunately, as I had previously noted, I later made the mistake of not always referring to that precise name of the estate in a future transaction with a company that provided royalty revenue. This led to some tax ramifications in the tax returns I filed for the first year of the estate. Clearly, I should have been very careful to use precisely the same name as on the EIN message.

Tip: Use the precise estate name as on the EIN message in any tax-related interactions.

Once we set up the new account for online banking, because I was not sure if any particular branch would be open in the future due to the virus. I ordered a starter set of checks, again thanked the person who helped me and walked out. (In retrospect, I should have ordered more checks, because the revenue streams are still going strong four years later and I expect the estate to collect royalty revenue for many years.)

After I received an EIN for the estate, I asked the paralegal working for my attorney for assistance and she was able to get the balance on the PayPal account sent as a check payable to the estate. As I later found out, I could have dealt with PayPal directly. They have great customer service by phone, or at least did so in 2021. Later, the paralegal was able to set up accounts for two international companies that were providers of royalty revenue streams, StreetLib and Immateriel.fr. (immateriel.fr[1] was the company that had been paying using PayPal.)

My experience with the second bank was much more difficult, and much less pleasant. In recent years, there had been two branches within about a half mile from my home. (There had been four such branches about twenty years ago.) Neither of the two aforementioned nearby branches had remained open during the height of the Covid-19 epidemic unlike bank #1.

Finally, the branch nearest to me opened for business again. I went inside and there was a single person working behind the low wall separating tellers from customers. I explained what I needed and she told me that she was the only one working there that day and did not know how to address the problem I needed solved. She looked up some company information and told me where I could find a branch that had people that could have taken care of my banking request. The branch was a bit too far away for me to walk and parking was going to be difficult. I checked the second branch near me and they had a sign on the door saying that the branch would be closing permanently and that anyone wishing to clean out their safe deposit box should call this number. Wow!

I called that number and hoped to get an appointment to empty out my safe deposit box. The number did not work. Wow! And Wow!

I finally found another telephone number on the bank's primary website that listed another number to be used to make an appointment to clear out safety boxes. I made the appointment and was able to get into our safe deposit

---

1.   http://immateriel.fr

box. I then carried all the essential information and the rest of the box's valuable contents to our nearby home.

All this was done at a time when it was not clear how much in-person banking will be available conveniently in the future, or even at all. A Maryland state senator was so concerned that the city of Baltimore was going to have so many of its neighborhoods deprived of this essential service that she was trying to get a bill voted on by the Maryland state legislature to allow what is called community banking (aka not funded by large "commercial banks" with headquarters out of state) approved to offer service in the entire state. The bill did not come up for a vote in the Maryland state legislature, but you can see my concern.

I finally did get an appointment at the inconvenient branch of bank #2. Printing out a years worth of statements showed evidence of two income streams that were not indicated on any of the statements I had obtained from bank #1. Getting the printed statements from bank #2 went as smoothly as I expected. Also, as I had expected, there was no brokerage account.

One income stream was from a Canadian firm called Kobo that was a direct purveyor of ebooks. Kobo recently had been taken over by the large Japanese conglomerate Rakuten. Kobo always paid ebook royalties monthly within a fixed period after the books were sold, provided the royalties exceed $50. According to the terms of agreement as a publisher, royalty payments might be delayed until the $50 minimum is achieved. Kobo payments seemed to be paid every month.

The second was from a company you have probably heard of — Apple. Apple's royalty payments were made monthly, reflecting that Apple always pays ebook royalties monthly within a fixed period after the books were sold.

Setting up the estate account at bank #1 had taken only a few minutes once the EIN was created for the estate.

It was clear that closing the existing account and setting a new estate account at bank #2 was going to take much longer, because neither of the bank personnel that I was working with seemed to understand what the correct procedures were. And they seemed to be the most knowledgeable personnel there.

Obviously, I had little confidence with the training and capability of the personnel I worked with at bank #2. I was not even sure that the bank would keep any full-service locations open in the city. (They did, but hindsight is always correct.)

The problems I ran into at bank #2 were so frustrating that I was even convinced that I should close that account. Two hours was too long to wait! I was working under the assumption that moving revenue streams to another account would be easy. I was wrong! Remember the old adage: "Act in haste, repent at leisure." It took a lot of work to get all the old royalty revenue and create a new revenue stream directly from Kobo and I have not been able to get either one directly from Apple, due to Apple's strict privacy rules although I am still hopeful.

From a revenue standpoint, my rash action did not matter, because any additional revenues sent from Apple to that bank account after my son's death would have been clawed back until a new account for the state would have been created, according to stated Apple policies and, of course, federal tax laws.

Tip: Don't close bank accounts too quickly. Wait a while until you fully understand revenue streams.

At this point, I need to do a shoutout to Shelley Adina who is a well-known author in a variety of genres. On her blog she described the procedures that many of the major booksellers, including Amazon, Apple, Barnes and Noble, Kobo, and Draft2Digital used when handling the royalties due to a deceased author. (Draft2Digital is an aggregator, similar to the companies StreetLib and Immateriel.fr that I had been dealing with.) The name of a contact person at Kobo was very helpful in what was a complex process. Thanks again. A link to this blog post is given in the references. Check https://ShelleyAdina.com to see all the information provided on her website. Her advice was most useful for authors rather than those who were publishers, but her rationales for her thinking was incredibly helpful.

My experiences with bank #3 were difficult, but for a different reason than what I had to deal with at bank #2. At the time I first checked, bank #3 had headquarters in Puerto Rico, with branches in Florida and New Jersey, but nowhere else in the United States. This seemed very odd to me. Why deal with a bank with headquarters in Puerto Rico when you have memories of a run on a bank as a teenager? Then I remembered, that my had considered moving to Puerto Rico to take advantage of the tax breaks available there.

There was another possibility, however. He had lived in Florida at one time and there was a branch location near to where he had lived. Perhaps he had had an account there.

(During the height of the Covid-19 epidemic, it was often illegal to travel out of state for nonessential reasons. So, there was no possibility that I could go to a bank branch in person.)

In any event, I called the number for the bank location that nearest to his former residence in Florida. I spoke to someone in customer service and she informed me that the account had been closed.

But was the account really closed? If so, why was there a debit card for that bank in his wallet? Perhaps he didn't bother cleaning out his wallet regularly. I simply don't know. As stated above, at the time that I checked this bank, it was impossible to travel to other states because of quarantines set up during the height of the pandemic. So, there was no trip from Maryland to Florida or to New Jersey to meet any bank personnel in person.

My decision was to let the matter be and simply wait for any funds that might have been in that bank to revert back to the state after a certain number of years had passed. Such missing money funds due to a person or entity that have reverted to a state for lack of use can be found at two wonderful websites that are discussed in a later chapter in this book.

Custodial Accounts

In this chapter, we will describe custodial accounts in general, although none of the typical issues were applicable in this particular case. In general, it is always possible that a minor child of a deceased person may have been the recipient of a custodial account having been set up. In some cases, the minor child may have been automatically designated as the recipient after death of a parent. In other cases, the surviving parent may have access. All possibilities should be checked. The most likely starting points are the bank offices at which the deceased had an account, since many physical banks required an actual visit to set up an account. Of course, this assumes that any such bank branch office is still open!

If there is no physical branch location, try to access information by using a website to locate phone numbers. Any organization that has the authority to have custodial accounts in a state will have both a website and phone access.

Many custodial accounts are set up using the Uniform Gifts to Minors Account standard. In Maryland, using the world "Maryland" as a prefix leads to the acronym MUGMA. This type of account helps shield a minor from some taxes and ownership of the account changes to the child upon attaining the official age of adulthood. (In Maryland, the ownership changes at age 21; check your own state's website for additional information.)

Another kind of custodial account is intended to help pay for college or other educational expenses, including private schools. Parents and grandparents (and possibly some other related people — check your state for more information) may donate funds for educational purposes free of state and local taxes. These so-called 529 plans are administered by most states either directly or through a large brokerage firm. In Maryland, two different types of such plans exist.

One type of plan simply keeps the donated funds in a tax-free account whose investment strategies become less aggressive and, hence, more conservative as the minor approaches normal college age. The value of a fund and its relationship to tuition at any selected college can be seen easily, on a regular basis. Information is available either via a website or by US mail.

A second type of plan uses a somewhat different mix of aggressive and conservative strategies to donated funds to effectively pre-pay tuition at state schools. It is not clear what happens if the beneficiary of such a plan does not quality for admission to his or her school in Maryland.

In Maryland, both are administered by T. Rowe Price, a large Maryland brokerage firm. Access to those accounts, is by telephone or by setting up an online account, at least in Maryland.

Get Access to Computers

The next thing I did was make a serious attempt to get information from the two laptop computers that my son had owned. I'll begin this chapter by describing a successful data recovery effort that happened about twenty years ago. Then in the next few sections, I'll discuss the difficulty in doing the exact same thing today due to changes in hardware and software technology but instead will describe a simple solution that works. Finally, I'll discuss the solution I actually used in this case. The intent of the discussion is to illustrate the things that can actually be used by an ordinary estate administrator to access nearly any computer's data.

Tip: It is possible to get access to a computer's data files by connecting its disk storage to another computer using a USB-based connector.

A Case Study From the Nineties

As stated above, I had done this type of data recovery myself about twenty years ago, when a friend at the local genealogical society asked me for help recovering his data from a computer that would no longer boot up. His 1995-era laptop had died and he had a draft of a nearly complete book of transcriptions that he wanted to publish. So, he wanted the data on this non-working machine. I talked to people at the Geek Squad desk in a local Best Buy and they said they could do recover this data at a cost of $50 per hour. Remember that this was twenty years ago, so doing the same thing probably would be more expensive today.

I knew that the two most common problems with the failure of the computers of that time to boot up were having a corrupted disk or else having a failed power supply. The failed power supply problem was the more prevalent one affecting PCs, so I decided that all I needed to do was to look at the disk. I described to my friend what I wanted to do to his computer in a non-destructive manner and he agreed that we should proceed.

Most laptops of that time were easy to open with a standard sized Phillips head screwdriver so I knew that I could open this one and remove the 3.5 inch drive. That drive was magnetic, unlike the solid state memory that is most commonly used in newer computers. I unplugged the computer, removed the internal screws, then went to a small computer store and explained what I wanted to do. They sold me a standard enclosure for a 3.5 inch hard drive magnetic disk that I would place the old disk drive in, and, in turn, would be powered by connecting the enclosure's USB cable to a USB port of a newer computer of my own.

The first step was to turn off my own computer. I placed the old computer's magnetic disk into the new enclosure I had bought, then plugged the enclosure's cable into a USB port in my own computer. I then turned my computer on and could see my friend's folder that contained all my friend's files, both ones with his data, and other ones used by the operating system or used to run applications such as browsers and *Microsoft Word*. My computer had a CD drive, so I copied all my friend's data files from that folder onto a CD. There was no point to copying the operating systems files, or the files used in any of the applications that were on his computer because it was so old that none of those applications would work on any newer computer.

Fortunately, a potential technical problem did not arise in this particular circumstance. Both my computer and my friend's were windows-based PCs, and therefore they used the same type of file system. The way that files were stored had changed over time, especially in the early days of personal computing because files got larger. The earliest operating Microsoft operating systems were designed for what were called 16-bit computers, and the maximum size of any file was severely limited. Later computers had a newer organization of file systems, which might have led to chaos when trying to read files from my friend's computer using my own. I hadn't thought about this potential problem at the time; I just got lucky. I would have needed some special software and perhaps other technical assistance.

I did a quality check on the two sets of files, the one I had copied to the CD and the one on the old disk to see if all the files were there, and if each of the files was the same size. I then ejected the CD and turned off my computer.

While my computer was off, I removed the enclosure's USB cable from my computer. How much did it cost? Less than fifteen dollars and I had a usable disk enclosure that I might be able to use again.

I put my friend's old computer back together and left him with the problem of recycling it. I did suggest to him that he use a powerful magnet to scramble the data on his old laptop, or even take a hammer to it for data security and privacy reasons.

I was glad I had not taken my friend's computer to a company where a technician would work on it. One of the files I found was a tax return! I could trust myself, and my friend could trust me, and no unknown technician would be able to look at files. In any event, the problem was solved.

You should note four things from this discussion.

1. Once I had connected the two computers and getting both computers to power up, my own and my friend's, I was able to read every file on my friends computer by booting up mine, viewing all the files stored on the disk on my friend's machine as just another set of files on a remote disk.
2. I did not need a password to get access to files on the computer disk I wished to search.
3. I chose to not copy files used by the operating system or any application programs.
4. I could have copied all the the files used by the operating system or any existing application programs on the computer I wished to search. The only technical reason for not doing so was the lack of room on the computer that I was temporarily transferring files to, especially since I expected to download files to CDs which had relatively small capacity.

The most important thing to take away from the discussion of these four issues is that, once you were able connect the device that stored the files on the computer you wished to search to the power coming from your computer, the data transfer probably would almost certainly be easy to accomplish. You'll see that there might even be an easier, low-tech way to transfer the desired data in many circumstances. We'll look at several possible methods, ranging from simplest to hardest.

The Simplest Possible Solution

The simple process that I am describing here is to just connect a cable between my Mac desktop and my deceased son's two PCs, one PC at a time, and read the files on each one in turn.

The cable would have to match the PC on one end, with some version of a USB or USB-C cable and the Mac, which used a Lightning connection to connect on its end. I did not do this, because I had no way of knowing just how large the totality of data was on my son's computers. Would there be so much data that I could not transfer all of it? Or, would some of the data be overwritten? Also, I wanted to keep my son's data separate from the personal data that was already stored on my own computer if a legal problem about the estate arose.

I actually arranged to use the same company that had sold me the enclosure I had used for transferring my friend's data to a CD. I purchased a large-capacity portable disk with cables and had them do the transfer. It was cheap. Even if the cable transfer would have worked, I wouldn't have saved much money, because I traded in the two unneeded PCs for the cost of the effort to transfer the data and the portable disk that I had purchased.

I would have to be very careful, since I did not know how much data was stored on my deceased son's PCs and I might not have been able to copy all the files. In that case, I would have needed a portable hard disk for storage, any how.

My recommendation to you is to try the simple cable connection first. It won't cost more than about $12 even if you have to buy a cable. Once you see how much data you need, you can buy a portable disk for storage.

The obvious question is why I didn't just buy a cable and to connect a cable first. The answer was simple — I was just beginning my grief process and I wanted to get the data from the computers. My memory is not as good as it once was and I jumped at the first solution I came up with.

Trying the Same 1990s Technique in Modern Computers

I knew that the technique that I used on my friend's computer would work with any computer that had a relatively large capacity magnetic disk. Unfortunately, that obsolete type of storage medium is rarely available on newer computers, especially newer laptops.

How does that long-ago experience apply to the problem of getting into my son's computers? The primary relevance is that, in many cases, you can get access to nearly any computer's user-created files without knowing any passwords. It is the same basic idea — use another computer and find a way to physically connect the "disk" of the computer you wish to get into to your own.

Here are the problems you might have.

- Modern computers are much smaller physically and any ordinary Phillips head screwdriver is probably much too large to fit. You probably need a jeweler's screwdriver.

- Many modern computers don't have 3.5 inch drives, but use what are essentially solid state chips. It is hard both to identify these chips and connect them to other devices.

- The internal dimensions of modern laptops are small and require great coordination, which I certainly do not have at my advanced age, is needed to work with them.

- Electronic devices are highly susceptible to static electricity, which can ruin them. Be sure to to be grounded, either by using an anti-static mat or a connection to a ground.

I did not think that I was able to do the physical transfer of the disks, so I was looking for an alternative.

I had seen several suggestions on various online tech forums about how to solve my problem of data transfer from a Windows-based computer, but these suggestions seemed rather complex and I was not sure that they would work. There were ads for services, and for software that purported to solve this problem, including one website of a particular software package that my computer flagged as insecure. None of these potential solutions seemed appropriate. So I looked for a better alternative.

There was an additional issue for me to consider. I have a Macintosh desktop computer with a large monitor that I had planned to use to compare online catalogs of publishers side-by-side to make sure that there were no duplicates. I needed a large amount of screen real estate to see essential information! My son's two laptop computers were Windows-based PCs. The technical problem I was worried about, with different organizations of file systems, might have arisen in this situation. (Apple had recently changed file system organization and memory management in some ways due to upgrading from a 32-bit processor to a 64-bit processor in its most recent products.)

The Actual Solution Used

I had considered but then eliminated several options to try to transfer the data files: take the computers apart working with small parts, use a software technique that I did not completely understand and was not sure it would work. Therefore I made an executive decision to ask the same company I had talked to in the past to transfer all the files from both of these laptops to a format that could be read by a Mac. I did trust the company, but knew that they would be able to see all files, including confidential ones. There was a risk, but I decided it was worth taking. I would have had the same vulnerability using a person recommended by the attorney.

In actuality, I was less concerned about the honesty of the company I was going to use, than about what I would do if either of the computer disks were encrypted. Getting files from an encrypted disk requires tremendous computer forensic skills, and was far too complicated for me or anyone I knew to help with easily. You've probably seen many television shows and movies where someone gets into a computer by finding a way to decrypt the data. (Movie directors seem to believe that watching someone type on a keyboard is exciting to watch. It is not.)

So I went to the same company I had dealt with before when I had been able to copy my friend's files, carrying two laptops and copies of the letters of Administration so they would be assured that I had a legal right to get the data.

Fortunately, the company was able to transfer all the files to a portable one-terabyte disk drive that I could connect to my Mac. I could open and read all the user-created data files.

I could also also see all the files of the operating system and applications, so, even if I could not use any of the PC-based files, I would be able to look in the directories for any confidential files that my son may have placed there.

Some people save cryptocurrency "wallets" under different names deep inside folders that normally are part of some applications. There might have been some other hidden files. I haven't found any such files yet, but I am continuing my search.

Use Biometrics For Access?

Many modern computers, as well as smartphones and tablets, allow their users to get access by using some form of biometric technology, such as Face ID and Touch ID that can be used on Apple devices. If you watched enough CSI -type shows, you might think that you could lift a fingerprint from a hard, flat surface using powder and a piece of transparent tape, then place it over the touch pad and you get access. This doesn't work.

Here's why. A fingerprint is stored internally by Apple and some other companies as a collection of whorls, ridges, arches, and tented arches, together with their relative positions, similar to the way that it might be compared to fingerprints in the FBI database. There are protections against just this possible attempt to break in. A small electrical circuit is created by a live person touching the screen that on which touch control can be used and such a current is required for access.

There are protections against placing, say, a picture of a person's face against a screen and getting access that way. As was true before with Touch ID, getting access using a picture using Face ID will fail, because of the way that facial images are stored with other metadata about the stored facial image. As before, a small electrical circuit is created by a live person and such a current is required for access. Find an identical twin and you might be able to get in.

NOTE: New AI techniques may negate some of these security measures. I have already been targeted with the well-known "grandson is in jail and needs to be bailed out" scam, which used a voice that I found to be indistinguishable from an actual grandson. Clearly the voice was generated by AI. Settling on a code word is a way to prevent being taken in by such scams.

You Have Access. What Can You Find?

When you have obtained access you can look at the files in the deceased person's computer. The combination of the organization of the files into the various folders and the names of the folders probably gives suggestions as to where what was there. But there is some additional information that can make your life as an estate administrator much easier. In the remainder of this chapter we list the two types of files that are most likely to help you in managing the estate: tax returns and emails.

Tax Returns

Tax returns are the easiest types of files to find, because you simply have to search for particular types of files, and the names of these types have specific extensions based on the tax preparation software used to create the return. Such files may even be stored in a folder name "tax" or similar. Fortunately, the information you need to find old tax returns on a Mac or a Windows PC is identical regardless of the computer..

Of course, the file name extensions of different commercially available tax programs will generally be different, depending on which brand of tax preparation software was used to create them.

For example, files created in recent versions of *TurboTax* will have their names end in the eight characters ".taxYYYY" where the YYYY is the year in four digits. *TurboTax* is the most commonly used commercial brand of tax return software.

A second major brand of tax preparation software is *TaxAct* which was developed for the well know company, H & R Block. *TaxAct* creates files with the four character extension ".tXX", where the XX represents the last two digits of the year.

There are other tax preparation packages, but I am not familiar with them. They probably use similar naming conventions.

If you can find a tax return file created in one tax preparation software package, but have another on your computer, and don't want to purchase a new one, do not worry. At least not too much. There is a standard that all packages are strongly encouraged to follow, known as Tax Exchange Format. Files created using this format will have the four character extension ".txf" and thus each tax prep software <u>should</u> be able to read them. At least that is the theory.

Of course, you can get copies of recent tax returns directly from the IRS. Abbreviated returns are free (at least currently) and more detailed ones can be obtained for a nominal price.

Email

The next topic we consider is email. We will discuss the wide range of types of email systems to help you understand what you might encounter and why email systems work the way they do. Some detailed suggestions of how to find email messages can be found in the remainder of this chapter.

Email access was one of the most difficult things I had to deal with during the early years of managing the estate. The difficulty was primarily due to the increasing emphasis on privacy by many of the companies providing email service, and how this emphasis conflicted with the needs of understanding and managing a digital estate.

As I mentioned earlier, I had saved all emails that my son had sent either to me or to his mother over the years. He used multiple accounts; some of the more recent ones used very strong end-to-end encryption and, thus, emails received in these encrypted accounts are not accessible. Of course, I could always tell what I had been sent to me, but it was hard, if not impossible, to see what email messages had been sent to or from him using other sources.

The solution is, of course, to make use of the fact that nearly all modern mailers keep records of the email messages sent and received, and keep them in the folders that they had been saved to. However, getting access to these messages can be very difficult and quite time-consuming, as we will see.

When I first used email in the 1980s, everyone in the School of Engineering at my university had a terminal in their office. Each of these terminals was connected to a departmental server that was connected to the outside world by a router. Email messages were text only, and were stored on the email server, with messages in your personal account stored there and displayed, but not saved on your personal terminal. With the advent of desktop computers, followed by laptops, along with networks and WiFi, there was no need to be hard-wired to anything and especially not to email servers. Companies that manufactured either computers or software, or both, such as Apple, Microsoft, and Hewlett-Packard began supporting email systems that could work remotely. Computer users took advantage of these capabilities. Email messages could be saved on personal computers!

Then companies such as Yahoo and Google developed their own email systems that worked everywhere. Apple's email could help manage multiple email clients, using Yahoo and Gmail within those mail applications.

Here's an extreme example. As stated above, the first email system I ever used was based on a server in the Computer Science department. Later, the entire university developed a campus-wide email system. That's two accounts that I had to log into, departmental, and university.

When I needed more reliable and faster email service, I created an account in Yahoo mail. I now had to log into three accounts. I could keep the webpage with Yahoo account open and log into one or another university account as necessary. I had a *Hotmail* account for a few weeks, but at that time, Microsoft typically closed these accounts after four days of non-use, so I went back to having only three email accounts. I currently use neither of the university emails, having let them go dormant after getting tired of having to constantly change my password for security purposes.

I created a Gmail account to have seamless transitions to Google apps. This makes four accounts.

I created two different email accounts for two web-based businesses that I run. I have to manage these mail server from the hosting company that I use. That's six email accounts.

The remaining account is the one I use to handle essential transactions on the estate account I set up. That's seven accounts, two of the dormant.

Obviously, it is far more efficient to use an overall email server application that accepts multiple accounts and puts mail in the appropriate folders. The one I chose to use is Apple's mail app, which works well.

All modern mailers keep track of your emails on your computer. This is much more efficient than reloading lots and lots of data every time you check your inbox.

My own experience illustrates several types of email systems you might have to deal with when trying to get access to emails from the deceased. You may have files from multiple mailers, and the accounts may be grouped by the overall mail app such as Apple's email app.

Old emails <u>from</u> my son to me provided useful information. I have already mentioned the happy email that he sent, saying he was back in the print business and forwarding a message that had been sent by StreetLib. I used this information to leverage access to other email accounts.

Even if one or more of the aforementioned email accounts were closed, I could make inquiries of certain companies, if they had a contact with anyone with an email address I gave to them. This allowed me to find out which, if any, of the email accounts had been used as, say, user names, and also Apple ID or Google ID.

As stated before, old email addresses may have served as Apple IDs on a Macintosh computer, so determining that there was an email address is important.

We'll break our discussion of searching old email addresses into two parts, one for a Macintosh and the other for a windows-based PC.

I'll start with Macs. I found some information on www.LifeWire.com/find-and-open-stored-attachments-1172808[1] to be incredibly helpful, because there is a non-intuitive step that is necessary to find email folders. This website states that the process is intended for people using Apple Mail with specific email accounts set up within it, which is exactly the way I have set up email on my Mac. Here are the steps:

1. Open a Finder window on your Mac.
2. Press the Option key near the bottom of the keyboard and hold it while selecting Go from the top menu bar. Press the Option key to see the Library. (The Library folder is not visible without pressing the Option key.)
3. Select Mail
4. Open folder V2. It shows some Mail data.
5. Open a folder named V10 (your computer may show a slightly different number as part of the folder name.
6. Many folders with long, complicated names will appear. My Mac showed seven mail folders, but your number may be different.
7. Look for the .mbox extension.
8. Search for whatever message you want.

The process for a Windows-based PC is apparently more complex than searching Apple Mail on a Mac, at least in some cases. A chat session on the topic of email storage of *Hotmail* messages on the website answers.microsoft.com[2] showed 13 replies, with a lot of technical angst demonstrated. I did not need anything from that location, because I was certain that he had never used *Hotmail* as a mailer.

More information can be found on multiple Internet forums, both ones sponsored and hosted by Microsoft, and others. Do a search for something like "where is email stored in Windows" for more information.

My son had changed email addresses frequently out of concern for privacy. Unfortunately, he had chosen Proton Mail as his last email service provider,

---

1.   http://www.LifeWire.com/find-and-open-stored-attachments-1172808

2. http://answers.microsoft.com

and and all messages sent to, or received from, this European-based mail service provider are entirely encrypted, so I could not read them.

Password Managers

A password manager is a piece of software that uses a single password (and perhaps other security mechanisms such as two-factor identification or physical site keys) to provide access to a file that holds all your passwords. Search the term "keychain access" on a Mac.

Look for one if you get access. This may help you with investigating websites and apps.

Brokerages, Retirement, and Insurance

I had already determined that my suspicion that there was no brokerage account associated with any of the banks my son had used was correct. Thus I determined that I only needed to search brokerages that were either entirely or primarily online. I didn't think he would have seen any value added to a brokerage with physical offices servicing customers face-to-face.

It was obvious that once I had found an online brokerage that he had used, I would have to provide definitive documentation proving that:

- My son was deceased. This required a death certificate.

- I was who I said I was (the Personal Representative and Administrator of the estate). I had papers for this purpose.

- I had the right to access the estate. As indicated above, I had papers for this.

- I had an address and other contact information for my son's ex-wife, who was the custodian of their minor child.

Tip: Don't send anything to a brokerage until they tell you there is a record of an account and that you should send it to them.

Before I made any phone calls, I made copies of all the relevant digital documents and placed these digital files in a new folder on my computer. I also combined every such file into a single PDF file in case a brokerage wanted the proof presented that way. If you are an Apple user, search the Apple website for instructions on how to combine multiple PDF documents into a single one. Apple creates such document in a standard application named *Preview*. If you can't do this, or get someone you trust to do it for you, you can proceed by sending copies of the documents either one at a time, or as multiple attachments to the same email, or on a USB flash drive by some very reliable delivery service. Don't send originals unless you have no other choice AND you have duplicates.

I decided to get some guidance as which of the brokerages I should search first. I went online and found a list of the top ten online brokerages in terms of popularity and used this as a starting point. I knew that I wanted to speak to real persons instead of using chat boxes, because my situation might have been too complicated for the relatively simple conversation that occurs within a chat box. Initially, I tried to avoid contacting online brokerages that were noted for having rather poor customer service.

(If I were doing this kind of search today, I would avoid using anything that used AI as much as I could, because I remembered something that I learned in a graduate course in artificial intelligence years ago — the difficulty that the AI-based expert systems of the time with their knowledge bases and their inference engines had in being widely adopted because there was no way to verify the choices of data to be evaluated by logical inferences. Potential liability issues concerned both the legal and insurance professions. The same problems exist today in large AI-based systems, even with the remarkable advances in using AI to generate interesting text.)

I found the following approach to get to a person in customer service who handles estate issues. Of course, these companies always have people who are very helpful and knowledgeable about almost any estate issues that might arise. Describe the situation using the words "deceased" or "bereavement." Have pencil and paper ready to write everything that you learn down. Be sure to get all contact information.

1. Introduce yourself and say "I am the Personal Representative and Estate Administrator of my deceased son *FirstName LastName* and I'd like to find out if he had an account with you. Can you tell me if he had an account if I gave you his Social Security Number?" (Don't give the Social Security number yet.)

2. The person who answers the phone will probably redirect your call. When you finally reach a person who handles such access, say "I was

directed to you and "I am the Personal Representative and Estate Administrator of my deceased son *FirstName LastName* and I'd like to find out if he had an account with you. Can you tell me if he had an account if I gave you his Social Security Number?"

3. As stated above, continue until you get an actual person who answers "yes." Then recite the Social Security Number.
4. If the answer is no, then thank them, and tell them you will check some other brokerages, and hang up.
5. If the answer is yes, they will probably tell you that there is something, but that they may not be able to provide further information due to obvious confidentiality issues.
6. Be sure to tell them that the deceased had died intestate and that information on anything held jointly with his ex-wife would be forwarded to her.
7. Ask them what information they want, and also ask if you can send it to them by email (assuming you were able to create the documents).
8. Repeat the instructions to deliver the necessary documents to make sure you have the right contact information.
9. Follow the instructions.

What did I find when I finally located a brokerage that had my son's accounts? I needed to know what to send before I sent the estate documents electronically? They told me that there were was an IRA and a stock account, both held jointly between my deceased son and his ex-wife, and a small sweep account designed to hold dividends from various stocks. The sweep account had no beneficiary and the value was less that $100; the amount was intentionally kept small because it simply was a place holder for dividends. They told me that I would get a package from them with forms that were to be filled out and the address that I was to send the entire package back to, all to be sent to the attention of the estate department.

Soon after, I received a package in the mail with three things: a sealed package concerning the joint IRA that was to be sent to my ex-daughter-in-law in order to be filled out by her and returned by her directly to the brokerage, a similar sealed package for the joint stock account with the same instructions, and a small check, presumably from the sweep account, that was to be deposited directly into the estate account by me as executor.

This was a wonderful way to handle things. I had completed all my responsibilities for the funds by hand-delivering the sealed packages to my ex-daughter-in-law. A joint IRA passes over outside the estate. She was the co-owner of the stock account, so that was outside the estate, also. An excellent solution, with money going to the proper place and me being removed of some responsibility.

The brokerage firm used excellent privacy practices and did not provide any detailed information on the size of the accounts. They kept this information private, reflecting the need for confidentiality. The amount of the joint IRA and brokerage account was none of my business.

Of course, you should check all the online brokerages you can in order to find any potential accounts.

Keep in mind that any accounts that are dormant for a long term can revert to the state. This means that, even if you miss contacting any particular brokerage in your first round of efforts, the funds therein will eventually end up being entered into a system for unclaimed funds, which you can access using either unclaimed.org[1] or the MissingMoney.com[2] websites that we will discuss in a later chapter.

The last thing to search for in this group is insurance policies. If there is a safe deposit box, or if you have paper records, simply call the number and get the claim forms. If you have no records, then begin a call process similar to what you did for brokerages. Note, however, that an insurance company may have changed its name at some time after the policy was issued. Some insurance company websites may list names of recently acquired smaller companies. You can also go a simple Internet search for any older name of a company.

I had none of these pieces of information. However, I did find an item on the MissingMoney.com[3] website for Maryland and actually visited the

---

1.   http://unclaimed.org

2.   http://MissingMoney.com

Maryland office that handled abandoned property. It was fifteen minutes drive from my house and there was inexpensive garage parking nearby. We'll discuss these websites in a later chapter.

---

3.   http://MissingMoney.com

Treasury Direct

Treasury Direct is the common name of the US government website treasurydirect.gov[1], where you can get information on treasury notes, bills, and bonds and also buy and redeem them. My experience with this website was influenced by the fact that my ex-daughter-in-law remembered that my deceased son had told her that he had bought some treasuries during their marriage. Therefore, I did not need to make a call to determine if there had been any purchase. I simply made the call in order to enable the estate to have control of those funds. Of course, I was assuming that none of these instruments had been redeemed already.

As was the case when making a claim to a brokerage firm, you may be asked to show evidence of you having an official Letter of Administration. If you are providing the claim documents entirely online, you may be asked to show that the document is official, in the sense that it has an official seal. If you only have only one copy with the seal, you certainly don't want to send it in to anyone.

I received some helpful advice from the US Treasury person who handled this claim. One helpful tip was to take a sharpened number two pencil and lightly move it over the seal on the official Letter of Administration document, in order to highlight the seal, highlighting the fact that it was an official document. After doing so, you can run an eraser, preferably a gum eraser of the kind you can buy from a stationery store or art-supply store, that you can move lightly over the document to remove any residue.

I was glad that I had a pencil and paper handy to take notes on the process, because it was at least as complicated as the process for getting access to funds held in an online brokerage.

Here was the process I followed. I got most of my information from a very helpful person who answered the phone when I reached the right area. As expected, I was asked for my deceased son's Social Security Number. The person told me the kind of treasury financial instruments that had his SSN on them, and how the ownership was set up. (Knowing the kind of treasury financial instruments gave a limited view into their value, but I was not told of the total amounts, for obvious privacy reasons.)

---

1. http://treasurydirect.gov

Conveniently, everything was to be done online. I was told what to submit, how to submit, and that I needed the seal on a Letter of Administration needed to be visible. (This conversation is where I learned the useful trick of highlighting the seal with a soft pencil.)

I gave the information to my ex-daughter-in-law along with some government forms since she would have to make the claim officially as next of kin.

The websites listed below provide websites for sending and receiving forms and other useful information.

Tip: Run a sharpened number two pencil lightly over an official seal on a document you are submitting.

The complete website address for the necessary and useful information is www.treasurtdirect.gov/indiv/indiv.htm[2]. Please note that websites get revised frequently to improve their usability, so the websites listed below may have been revised

Since the treasury bonds were electronic, I was also directed to www.treasurydirect.gov/email.htm[3].

I also was told that I needed to go to the website www.treasurydurect.gov/TH/THGateway[4]. There I would find a Form 1455A which would have to be filled out for my son's minor child to remain a beneficiary.

---

2. http://www.treasurtdirect.gov/indiv/indiv.htm

3.   http://www.treasurydirect.gov/email.htm

4.   http://www.treasurydurect.gov/TH/THGateway

Find Funds From MissingMoney.com[1] or Unclaimed.org[2]

The thought of finding money owed to you (or in this case, into an estate) is very appealing. However, you should know that finding the source of any claimable money is only the first step. Some potential funds may be just that, potential. The reason is that you may not be able to provide acceptable documentation. Let's consider the return of a security deposit on an apartment. If there is no copy of a lease, because the decedent didn't have paper records, there might not be any proof of residence. The same holds true for a security deposit. I think the best strategy is to do the search, but not try to make the claim unless you have reason to believe that the amount is worth it AND you think you have acceptable documentation. I'll address this issue again at the end of this chapter.

Tip: Make sure you have proof of residence before claiming money.

There is one other piece of advice that I can give to help you with documentation. When making a claim, you may be asked to show evidence of you having an official Letter of Administration. If you are providing the claim documents entirely online, you may be asked to show that the document is official, in the sense that it has an official seal. If you only have only one copy with the seal, you certainly don't want to send it in to anyone. You'll recall that I ran into this problem when working with the US Treasury to get access to some treasury instruments.

That helpful tip was to take a sharpened number two pencil and lightly move it over the seal on the Letter of Administration, in order to highlight

---

1. http://MissingMoney.com

2. http://unclaimed.org

that it was an official document. After doing so, you can then run an eraser, preferably a gum eraser of the kind you can buy from a stationery store, lightly over the document to remove any residue. We'll discuss the process of getting treasury bonds, notes, and bills in a separate chapter.

Tip: Run a sharpened number two pencil lightly over an official seal on a document you are submitting.

The website of the National Organization of Unclaimed Property Administrators has changed over the years. The organization now has a much more friendly and informative name for its website, www.unclaimed.org[3]. As of the writing of this book, that website is organized as follows.

There is a header briefly explaining what the purpose of the website is. This is followed by two ways to access the website's underlying search methods. We'll discuss each of these two ways in turn.

The first way to search is by clicking the left-most of three large icons, with the words "Find Your Property," which leads to MissingMoney.com[4], which is the only website that is endorsed by the National Organization of Unclaimed Property Administrators.

Enter the website's URL carefully, then double check before opening it. **Be careful not to visit commercial websites with similar names**. These other websites charge for services that are essentially free. Of course, there is always the possibility of scamming sites.

Searches can be done for a person's name, or for the name of a company. The default search is for everywhere in the United States and its territories. There are search fields to reduce the number of matches by entering a state, then even reduce the number of hits more by entering a city, and then by entering an amount range.

---

3. http://www.unclaimed.org

4. http://MissingMoney.com

Here are some examples. Searching this website for the pattern *FirstName LastName* of my deceased son's name states that there were 999 matches, but that may be a cut-off number of some much greater number. Restricting the to the state of Maryland leads to 195 matches, much smaller than what we got from the website. The first 5 matches have the correct *FirstName*, and match what is shown in the list of results below exactly. The address is correct, also.

We'll next look at Florida. There were 995 matches listed, which was reduced to 165 when his last known address was entered. This is a small enough number to make going through every hit returned. (The actual initial number of hits may have been higher than 995, which seemingly was the case the search in Maryland records.)

Our search for missing money in Puerto Rico showed exactly 2 hits, which is far lower that the number that was returned by a much broader search with, apparently, fewer restrictions.

Finally, we searched for Washington, DC. This search returned 158 matches, easily enough to return by an exhaustive search.

The second way of searching for unclaimed property on www.unclaimed.org[5] is by using an interactive map of the United States. This map is near the bottom of the home page of unclaimed.org[6]. Clicking on a state takes you to a website which allows searches for unclaimed property. Note that it is hard to search for a "state" such as Washington, DC, because it is hard to select that icon due to its small size.

When looking at the website in this way it seems as if the national organization decided that the best thing to do was to make the ability to search and recover available as quickly as possible for its users, and not try to have multiple meetings to select a single design of one interface, and then have all fifty states and several US possessions revise their working websites to conform.

Here's what that decision leads to. I'll describe what you would get for a person name of the form *FirstName LastName*, with no middle initial in

---

5. http://www.unclaimed.org

6. http://unclaimed.org

a few examples that are relevant to my personal situation as a Personal Representative.

In Maryland, there are two widely separated places where you can enter data, one for a first name and one for a last name. Looking for the *FirstName LastName* pattern for me, I found five hits, each with an associated case number. I found the case numbers hard to read, but there is a tiny arrow to the right of each case number that provides the case number displayed in a very, very large font. The case number leads to a form that can be filled out and submitted. This website has an excellent feature for reducing the number of hits — an address field is included.

Florida has a different, much cleaner interface on the website fltreasurehunt.gov[7], which allows searching for both *FirstName* and *LastName* and leads to a page that displays the last reported address. There were 22 hits. An excessive number of hits can be reduced by selecting a particular city.

Puerto Rico's website, ucfl.uscourts.gov[8], shows a way to search for any bankruptcy cases. There were 14,705 hits for that name combination and it was impossible to narrow it down without more information, such as funds being being created after a specific date, or debt greater than any minimal amount.

I looked at the website for Washington, DC, because it shares a border with Maryland. The website only allowed searching for *FirstInitial* and *LastName*. As you would expect, this leads to a huge number of hits.

I think it is pretty clear that using the first website recommended by the professional organization, MissingMoney.com[9], provides the simplest searches. Please note that clicking on a known match indicates what company or organization currently has the missing property and also indicates how to make a claim.

However, the Maryland site has at least one issue that can cause difficulty — how to submit documents. Like most states, Maryland is reorganizing many of the ways its citizens interact with their government, and is also phasing out the back-of-the-house storage in databases that used an ancient computer language, COBOL, that few, if any, colleges and universities teach today. In doing so, there may be quality control problems in user interfaces and in the

7.   http://fltreasurehunt.gov

8.   http://ucfl.uscourts.gov

9.   http://MissingMoney.com

methods of submitting necessary documents. The form that I used was obtained from the website www.marylandtaxes.gov[10].

Part C of the main document asks for supporting documents. An image is shown below. Notice that there is no mention of submitting a proof of address. Note also that there is no place to attach electronic copies of documents, so the package had to be send by some form of surface mail.

Part C - Provide the following documents

- [x] Copy of your driver's license or other ID (Required)
- [x] Copy of Social Security Card or other documentation containing social security number (Required)
- [x] Bank documents (e.g. passbook, bank statement, cancelled check)
- [x] Proof of affiliation with:
- [x] Letters of Administration   [x] Small Estate Papers   [ ] True Test Copy of Court Order
- [x] Copy of Death Certificate(s) for: xxx
- [ ] Other: ____

The last line of the firm states that the documents must be mailed to an indicated address.

Mail to the address located on the top of the claim form.

Since there have been multiple problems with the regular US mail service since the reorganization of the post office in the middle of 2020, and since I did not know if FedEx or UPS could deliver to the claims office, I decided to deliver the package of the application and all the required supporting documents by hand to that office. The office was a fifteen minute drive from my house and there was a garage about two blocks away. (I did not want to park at any nearby parking meters on the street, because I did not want to run out to feed the parking meter if I had to wait in line or was in the middle of a conversation with a clerk in the claims office.)

The major difficulty in processing was the claims office making sure that my deceased son was exactly the person to whom the unclaimed funds would be

---

10.   http://www.marylandtaxes.gov

released. In short, I needed to be able to show that my deceased son had once lived at the address that I found on the website. He had lived there for many years, so it was clear to me that it was the correct person. The issue was, how was I to prove it to the claims examiner when I had no proof with me, because none was asked for and, as I indicated at the beginning of this book, I had no paper records. There were five people with the same first and last names listed in my search for unclaimed funds in Maryland. Apparently, either a senior claims examiner gave approval on the basis of what was presented, or there was only one match of the middle initial, or, possibly another kind of record was found in another state database that I had not examined. I don't know what caused the claim to be approved, but I am convinced that going to the office in person helped. I am glad I lived close enough to the office to do so.

As I was leaving, the claims examiner told me that I could have sent in the forms electronically! Hmm.

One last thing. I got my claim accepted on November 29, 2023. I was told it would be about two months to process. I called the office on March 5, 2024 and was told that processing will begin in a few months and will take about six months after that! As stated earlier, the old systems were written in COBOL and are being replaced. Slowly, very slowly. (Maryland state tax refunds are also very slow this year, due to the software reengineering process.)

Get Access to Phones and Tablets

This chapter considers two wildly different types of phones: phones that can be considered smartphones and, for lack of a better word, non-smartphones. Tablets have essentially the same software architecture as smartphones in the same product line family.

We use the term smartphones to mean any device such as *iPhone, Google Android*, and *Samsung Galaxy*. These types of smartphones are able to send and receive text message, make and receive phone calls, get email service, access the Internet, take photographs, play music and games, read books, and run a variety of apps on any of the major wireless carriers such as AT&T, Verizon and T-Mobile as well as some smaller service providers, Some models of these tablets do not use wireless carriers, but instead connect only using WiFi.

Most companies that produce smartphones also produce tablets that run similar versions of their smartphone operating systems and have similar capabilities, with the only major difference being screen size.

By non-smartphones, we mean the large class of far less expensive devices with more limited capability. Some in this category have only text and voice capability. Some have text, voice, and email. Others have four capabilities: text, voice, email, and Internet access. There are versions that are intended for those with limited vision or hearing. Makers of these types of phone and providers of their services include Jitterbug, Cricket, and Mint. These non-smartphones generally do not have an app store, where a user might have been able to install apps created by others in a smooth, seamless way. Any app stores that do exist are likely to be small.

Don't ignore the possibility that just having only access to a simple non-smartphone might be necessary to get access to a specific application that runs on a computer. Getting access to this phone might help with getting into a website that required getting a text message to enable the ubiquitous two-factor ID in order to be able to log into a website. You certainly cannot use two-factor ID if you cannot receive texts on the matching phone number that was originally set up for use with the account.

Before we begin an overview of the technical issues in getting access to any of these devices, it is important to consider if it will be worthwhile to do so at all.

How do you find out what's on these devices? The only suggestions I can make require you to have some knowledge of the deceased person's digital lifestyle. Here are a few things to consider before trying to get data from a smartphone. We will start with the easiest ones first.

• Do you know the passcode to the smartphone? My wife and I share the same passcodes on our iPhones. We have been married close to 60 years, so we trust one another.

• Do you know the deceased person's AppleID and password for their iPhone? An AppleID is an email address, probably the one that was first used when an Apple product was purchased. There are similar terms for email addresses on most other smartphones.

• Was a "legacy contact" set up and, if so, was it you? Apple was one of the first makers of smartphones to use the term "legacy contact" to describe a person who would be able to access everything via using your simple email address in the event of a death of a phone owner. Google and many other tech companies have followed suit, so that information should be searched for also. General non-technical articles about this topic can be found at nolo.com[1] and www.washingtonpost.com[2], among other places .

• Was cloud storage used? If so, can you arrange to make payments in order to have the cloud data remain available until legal questions about access can be solved?

• Was every photo or video taken on a phone downloaded to a computer that you have at least physical access to? If so, have you gained access to those files already?

---

1. http://nolo.com

2. http://www.washingtonpost.com

• Was the music stored on the phone or stored in the cloud? If so, have you gained access to those files already?

• Were there any ebooks stored on this phone, and, if so, are they stored in the cloud or on another device?

• Are there likely to be apps that will have had in-app purchases? If so, and you know the particular app, you might be able to get access to data by contacting the company that created the app directly.

• Does your lawyer, or any other lawyer you know, have a contact in a state where companies such as Apple and Google have their headquarters? Getting the approval of one of these two California-based companies is possible provided that the company has said in writing that they will accept a writ of a California court requiring them to allow you to access email records. Getting such a writ remotely is hard if you are the Administrator of a Maryland-based estate and live in Maryland and neither your or your lawyer do not have reciprocal legal contacts there. This is one of those times when dealing with a branch of a large company, in this case a legal firm, is better than dealing with a smaller one, because the larger company may have corporate offices in California.

I have found that it is much harder to get physical access to files on a smartphone or tablet than it was to do so on a computer, as we discussed earlier. You would either have the skills to disassemble a smartphone yourself and place the memory in a new phone carcass, or have someone who could do that for you. I don't think a typical technician in a mall will attempt to do that because of the questionable legality.

Several companies state that they have data recovery software for smartphones as well as for computers. Although I do not have enough specific technical experience to recommend any specific company in this book, it is appropriate to make some general observations on this issue. Many such companies have been in that business for many years, even since before the time that I wrote my simple introductory book on data recovery.

Here's my advice. Stay away from using any company that doesn't have both a stellar reputation on technical websites such as CNet and a careful process to make sure that any buyers of their software and service are careful to check that they have the actual rights to the data. If you are sending the phone away for data recovery, try to deal only with with a company in the same state as you if you can, just to provide for easier remedies in case legal issues arise.

Here's a reminder: Pay for months of cloud service even if you can"t access it at present. This buys you time for the court approval of your writ to be issued and get on the docket for a court. If the cloud payments stop, it will be harder to retrieve even if a favorable writ is finally issued. Of course, the time for a court to process and enforce a writ will depend on many things, including case backlog, so you should err on the side of caution when paying for cloud access even if you cannot use it.

Now we consider the question of getting access to any data stored in what we have called non-smartphones. As we discussed earlier, such phones tend to have at most the following four capabilities: text, voice, email, and Internet access. The most common arrangement is to have the first three features available. Judging by the frequent changes of email address, always in the direction of increased security and encryption. I did not believe that my deceased son would have risked the security of a single email account on a phone and, thus, would have chosen a carrier and phone combination that had only voice and text. Therefore, I decided that it wasn't worthwhile to pursue getting access to his phone any farther.

I did know that that getting access to call logs required a subpoena. I also learned from an online user forum that Cricket (his provider) did not keep logs of text messages, at least at the time that the person who responded to the query reported this finding. Since my deceased son's phone number was still in the *Favorites* list of my contacts app, I considered that issue as being solved.

Digital Currency and Digital Wallets

There are many types of digital currency in use today. Unfortunately, some sorts of digital currency have existed only for a very short time and, hence, it is not surprising that the laws to treat them have not completely kept place with some of the changes in the technology.

Let's start the discussion with some terminology. We'll present the most common usage, because the terminology has not been standardized.

The term "digital currency" means any currency, money, or money-like asset that is usually stored, managed or exchanged on one or more computer systems. Since an intermediary such as a bank or government is almost never used, these are called "peer-to-peer" connections.

A "digital wallet" is a place, usually a file or a file folder, or possibly an app, on a computer or perhaps even a smartphone, where access to a digital currency can be stored.

The term "cryptocurrency" refers to a special kind of digital currency that does not require any approval or management by any centralized organization such as a government or bank.

The term "blockchain" refers to the fully distributed technology that is intended to keep cryptocurrency transactions secure. It is far too complex to discuss here in any detail.

This chapter will also include a discussion of peer-to-peer transmission of money, for the purpose of consistency and inclusion. We list some such things below in groups.

Let's look at some ways to keep money on a smartphone, tablet, or even a simpler mobile device that runs software whose purpose is to enable transfers. You probably are aware of at least a few of them: Apple Wallet, Apple Pay, Google Wallet, Google Pay, Samsung Wallet, Samsung Pay, PayPal, Zelle, Venmo, and Xoom. This capability is in addition to traditional banks and credit unions having their own electronic banking systems.

The most common digital wallets in the United States are Apple Wallet, Google Wallet, and Samsung Wallet. They are useful to keep track of such things as electronic tickets to events, airline boarding passes, vaccine records, and identification cards.

Apple Pay works something like this. All the information that would ordinarily be stored the chip of a credit card or debit card is stored inside the device, usually an iPhone or iPad. You set this up by scanning your card in a few steps. Using Apple Pay instead of the swiping or tapping of a credit card lets the transaction go forward between you and the merchant, using encryption without exposing your credit card details to the merchant, which is the way that PayPal, among other services work. (Of course in many restaurants, the information on your credit card can be obtained before the information is transmitted over a presumably encrypted channel.) I note that in February of 2024, credit cards issued by Chase did not work on Apple Pay for approximately one day.

Although I have never used them, Google Pay and Samsung Pay have essentially the same level of functionality. The internal mechanisms of Apple Pay and Samsung Pay are somewhat similar to one another, with Google Pay using a slightly different mechanism.

These devices and their apps are all convenient. What happens when the owner of a smartphone dies and you, as executor of an estate, don't have access to the smartphone? Reread the chapter on accessing smartphones.

If you use any of these apps, be sure you have arranged for a legacy contact, or at least, shared the access code to be able to use the smartphone or tablet.

As stated previously, a cryptocurrency is a special form of digital currency that has no centralized control by a government or a bank. Two of the most commonly used cryptocurrencies are Bitcoin and Ethereum.

A cryptocurrency has several features that are purported to have multiple advantages over ordinary cash or money that is stored in banks and financial institutions. It is claimed to be inflation-proof, because there are only a fixed, limited number of such currencies available. It is supposed to be free from surveillance by government and hackers, because transactions are transmitted via what is generally considered a secure router, *tor*. (The FBI was able to trace the location and account of a graduate student at Harvard who used *tor* to disguise his making bomb scares during examination periods.)

A cryptocurrency is supposed to always increase in value, because the total number of them is fixed. However, that reasoning may not apply if the cryptocurrency is halved, as has been the case of Bitcoin several times. Think of halving as being the equivalent of stock splits.

It is not surprising that the question of getting access to a digital wallet is becoming a great concern. It is easiest if you have the passcode for, or are the legacy contact for, a device that belongs to a deceased person. On all Apple products, once a person has the passcode to the phone or tablet, or the password to a phone, they can get access to an area of System Settings that has all saved passwords. You can access the list of passwords on an Apple device by entering the passcode (for a phone or tablet) or the password (for a computer). Other devices *might* have similar features.

Recovery of cryptocurrency after a person dies without having a password or passcode to the entire device will be much more difficult than dealing with a bank, because of the completely distributed nature of the cryptocurrency.

It does appear that most companies that are active in cryptocurrencies have bereavement services, similar to those we described dealing with when we discussed getting access to funds in brokerage accounts.

What about access to a cryptocurrency such as bitcoin after a person's death? Here are two representative examples of the kind of general information that is available currently.

Coinbase is a company that provides crypto. It has a webpage: https://help.coinbase.com/en/coinbase/managing-my-account/other/how-do-i-gain-access-to-a-deceased-family-members-coinbase-account.

The website for stackexchange provides digital wallets for bitcoins has the following website information: https://bitcoin.stackexchange.com/questions/18663/recovering-bitcoins-after-the-owners-death.

Keep in mind that cryptocurrencies do not have the standard protections afforded by other, regulated financial institutions. Below, we describe two examples of protection provided by banks.

My wife and I were targeted by the well-known "my grandson is in jail and needs bail money to get out and I am afraid to tell my parents" scheme. We were almost convinced because we thought we recognized his voice. We had not expected such a "deep fake" AI-based attack and only determined that this was a scam when the scammers wouldn't accept a bank transfer but wanted to meet up with us and obtain actual cash. The amount requested was about $8800, under the usual limit of $10,000 that requires special approval by a bank manager. (My cousin's wife's uncle had been asked for $25,000 several years ago and only a bank officer's action prevented the cash from being handed to the crooks.

A second case that illustrates the importance of bank's protection was reported on the online news feed from *Business Insider* in a May 5, 2024 article. The title "Bitcoin trader loses $70 million after sending crypto to wrong address" of the article says it all. Of course, the trader had responded to an address of spammers. Beware.

Clearly, any major company that has any dealing with the management or storage of cryptocurrencies will have the ability to handle transfer of these currencies after a bereavement, although they not do so due to legal or other concerns. The problem that you are most likely to encounter is not having access to the actual account password. Since crypto accounts are hardly ever, or at least, not generally managed or serviced by a central authority, you really cannot expect much help. Every company has its own policies, so simply try your best to get help. It is possible that a crypto password is stored in a file that was deliberately placed inside a folder of the operating system or an application. Such a password probably wouldn't be much larger than 16 to 20 characters, so do a search for files of less than 20 bytes long.

You can get help on how to search your computer for files of that size. The useful answers will be written by a tech person and will probably be a program of no more than four lines long that can be typed into a terminal window on a Mac or on a PC. Good luck.

A password manager is a piece of software that uses a single password (and perhaps other security mechanisms) to provide access to a file that holds all your passwords.

A relatively new way to buy things over the Internet uses what are called "Non-Fungible Tokens," or NFTs. An NFT is essentially a digital image that can be watermarked in some fashion, so that copying that image, which is as simple as downloading a file, doesn't remove the value is based on the image's uniqueness. Finding access to a NFT also requires some technical calisthenics. Do an Internet search for "how to recover a NFT" for more information.

Social Media

Many people place a lot of information on various social media platforms. Users of Facebook (currently known as Meta) and Twitter (currently known as X), typically use them for the communication of information that is primarily intended to be of personal interest to the recipient or recipients. YouTube is used for many videos showing how to do certain repairs or to solve some technical channels. TikTok has videos that are much shorter in length than is typical of YouTube. (As this book is being written, it is not clear how long TikTok will be able to be available in the United StatesI am sure that many of this book's readers are considering archiving some or all of their TikTok videos. Finally, LinkedIn is used for business contacts and for networking.

I searched each of these websites for the following phrase "how to recover data from a bereaved person on ..." to discover the relevant policies of each of these social media platforms. Here's what I found when I searched the Internet on December 9, 2023, with few changes thereafter.

Facebook has an established policy for handling accounts of deceased persons. The current company policy is to "memorialize" the account to have its content always available, but have it locked against future changes, especially editing. There are separate paths for legacy contacts and for notifying Facebook about the death of a FaceBook user. This may be worth the effort financially for the estate, because of potential advertising revenue. The website explaining this is listed in the references but is presented here for convenience: https://www.facebook.com/help/275013292838654/?helpref=hc_fnav.

X has an established policy for handling accounts of deceased persons. The current company policy is to "deactivate" the account. The website is listed in the references but is presented here for convenience: https://help.twitter.com/en/rules-and-policies/contact-x-about-a-deceased-family-members-account.

TikTok seems to not have a formal bereavement policy at this time. The company website's help page is: https://support.tiktok.com/en. Keep in mind the possibility that TikTok may be banned, or at least restricted, in the United States

YouTube is a subsidiary of Google. The bereavement policy is essentially the same as Google's — get legal authorization. This may be worth the effort financially for the estate, because of potential advertising revenue. The website is listed in the references but is presented here for the reader's convenience: https://support.google.com/accounts/troubleshooter/6357590?hl=en.

LinkedIn has a policy somewhat similar to Facebook's in that the account of a deceased person can be "memorialized." The potential financial value to the estate is probably in locating business contacts. The website is listed in the references but is presented here for the reader's convenience: https://www.linkedin.com/help/linkedin/answer/a1336663.

Websites and the Wayback Machine

Almost any business, especially a digital business, will have a website. But where is the website, and how can you access it? There really are two possibilities: either the website is currently active, or it is not. If the website is still active, you can make sure the hosting company is still getting paid using the information available on the deceased person's computer. Keep in mind that there almost always are two kinds of things that must be paid — the fee for registration of the domain name and the company that hosts the domain's website so that users can see it.

There are several issues that arise if a website is no longer active. An inactive website created by the deceased for his or her company may have been taken down by the website's hosting company, if they were no longer being paid by the owner. If you can find the name of the former hosting company, you can contact them and, hopefully, they have archived that website, and can restore it once the back payments are made and new payments are arranged for the next billing periods. I find it easiest to search the official place for managing names of websites, which is icann.org[1]. The URL for the lookup is lookup.icann.org[2]. There are many companies that can provide this lookup service free of charge. These companies can provide other services, including hosting websites if the need arises. It is not difficult to migrate from one hosting service to another, if you so desire.

(One of the websites my son's business had used will have its registration expire on 9-12-24 and a second one will expire 10-10-24. In each case, I have found the name and contact information for the hosting company that is provided in the record. The hosting company is nationally known and appears to be unlikely to go out of business soon.)

Older websites, even defunct ones, often can be found at the Wayback machine that is hosted on the non-profit Internet Archive. It is located at https://Wayback.archive.org. (Older readers may recall a television cartoon

---

1.   http://icann.org

2.   http://lookup.icann.org

series that ran as part of the Rocky and Bullwinkle Show, with a man named Mr. Peabody, who, together with his boy, Sherman, could set the Wayback machine to any date in history.)

The Wayback machine is a volunteer effort intended to preserve digital culture. Since websites are constantly, changing, the Wayback machine samples them with the frequency of sampling related to the frequency in which changes occur.

Looking at an older snapshot in time of the website, I could see that one of my son's professional websites had not had any significant changes in a while. I could tell that there was a lot of content and most of the links on the main page worked to accurate contact. The website was organized into three primary columns, with a top banner covering the entire width of the screen on my laptop, and with occasional information in larger print on the right and left sides of the three content-filled columns. I believe this was an elegant design for viewing on a computer screen, and it looked like the design of a webpage that was done by a former user interface designer at Apple. (I had used the same three-column layout on a website of my own, but I have not revised it for a mobile device.)

I tried the same search on my smartphone and I saw a lot of errors when the main page was shown. What was the problem? Most modern websites use a relatively recent HTML standard that allows them to be shown on on many devices of different dimensions by having the webpage width set not as a fixed number of pixels, but automatically as a fraction of a HTML variable called *page_width*; this value is read by a typical browser used on the device. This means that even if I transferred all the files on the website, I would have to edit them individually, changing the width of each page. THAT is a back-burner project.

Can a snapshot of an entire website that is archived on the Wayback machine be archived? Yes, but you may need some help from experts. For example, a search for "download from wayback machine" shows the use of a powerful utility program called *wget* that you put in the address search bar in the same place you entered the domain you were looking for, then some special data to show parameters, then the domain you want. This is not for the faint-hearted, and a YouTube video may help. Good luck.

Businesses

By this point you should have developed a good understanding of the kind of business your deceased relative had done. There are some basic questions you need to answer before you proceed with running the business.

- Is the business a money-making one or is it just a hobby?

- Is the income produced sufficient to make continuing to run it worthwhile?

- Does the business have a name?

- Where are funds for purchases sent to the business stored? This place could be a bank, a payment managing company such as PayPal, or, perhaps even a cryptocurrency. (Since cryptocurrencies tend to be preferred on the dark web, be careful if you are trying to retrieve any information on the dark web. I'd be very, very, very careful before searching the dark web.)

- Is the business a corporation, a partnership, an LLC, or a sole proprietorship?

- If it is a corporation, where were the papers filed and who are the officers?

- If it is a partnership, who are the partners?

- Is the business primarily a service? If so, are there any outstanding services that the business had already agreed to provide, but had not provided?

- If the business is primarily a seller of products, have all sales requests been fulfilled?

• Does the business have a physical inventory that needs to be accounted for?

• If the business provides digital products only, what are the outlets in which it is sold?

• Are there any outstanding bills that are owed by the business?

• Are there any payments that are due to the business but are unpaid?

• Is the business entirely US-based, or is there an international aspect.

• What is the present value of the business? In other words, how much could you sell the business for? This could be important, considering my own rather advanced age.

Determining the present value of the business could be important, considering my own rather advanced age. I believe I have identified the income streams still coming into the estate. My current plan is to simplify the business, then create a video of the actions that have to be taken for the rather complex processes of creating and submitting invoices to each of the international companies used by my deceased son's business, and making sure my ex-daughter-in-law has access to the estate's bank account for my minor granddaughter. Of course, I would give the training videos to my minor granddaughter if she attains the age or majority while I am still alive. (Actually, I am creating multiple videos, because the invoicing procedures of the Italian company, StreetLib.com[1] and the French company, immateriel.fr[2] are so different.)

We note that old tax returns can be helpful in learning about businesses, because they often will indicate payment sources. If there are a few companies that provide income to the decedent's business, they should be listed on Schedule C. We note that the simple, abbreviated, tax returns you can get sent to you electronically for free often don't have all the information about the

---

1. http://StreetLib.com

2. http://immateriel.fr

business you might need, so you may need detailed tax returns, which, as stated previously will require a fee. An article by Susan Tompor in the March 12, 2024 issue of the *Detroit Free Press* (reprinted in *USA Today)*, has additional information.

International businesses can be especially difficult to understand because of language understanding issues. Many websites of international companies have an option that allows, at least, the opening page of the website to be translated to English. Most popular browsers have an option to translate, and this is often done on a page-by-page basis. I found that my slightly below performance in high school French that I took in the 1950s was adequate to understand everything I needed to know about a business relationship with a French company.

To summarize, one of the most important activities you can perform at this point is learning as much as you can about the nature of the deceased person"s business and using this information to guide your actions as estate administrator.

Sources of Income - Revenue Streams

Up to this point, we have discussed the fundamentals of management, responsibilities of the estate Administrator, that can be applied to any estate that has been created in the digital age. We have also discussed businesses in general.

It is now time to consider the specifics of the business that I needed to understand in order to be able to provide the best service I possibly can to my deceased son's estate. (I have alluded to the nature of this business earlier, but it is now time to discuss the issues in more detail.)

The best way to describe his business is as being primarily a book publisher. Early in his career, he had published a number of titles of lesser-known classics, but left that market when carrying a large physical inventory was no longer profitable. He spent a lot of time in libraries, and used that time to create some books that he was able to publish. On one occasion when I visited his booth at the Baltimore Book Fair, I was surprised to find that his primary cover designer was the great-great-grandson of a former United States Congressman who had represented our district in Congress for many years.

In a later effort, he had had a contract with the U.S. Marines to provide CDs of ebooks.

Some time after, he had moved his business almost entirely away from print books into the ebook market, selling both on his own websites and also on Amazon and, later on, Apple, Barnes & Noble, and Kobo. Much of his catalog was also available for sale in the bookstores associated with the now-defunct *Franklin eBookMan* and *Sony Reader* devices.

He may have also published ebooks on Google Play, but that portion of the Google empire was closed to new publishing content in 2015, and was reopened to new content in 2018. A Wikipedia article on Google Play Books describes the issues affecting multiple publishers and millions of ebooks. During that interval he was going through a messy divorce, and was looking for a more stable publishing platform. I saw no signs of any of my son's ebooks having been published to Google Play in any years more recent than 2018.

I did not look at the catalogs of any other of the now defunct ebook publishers, believing that no substantial royalties would have been paid because these publishers had insufficient inventory.

Since the market for his catalog had changed away from physical books to ebooks, he stopped going to those book fairs where vendors expected to sell many books to individual book buyers, and instead went to both national and international book fairs, where he made professional contacts. He spent most of his time at those fairs networking, speaking to both national and international authors and publishers. He took over the process of digitizing some older and classic books into meeting modern standards for ebooks that could be read on multiple devices unlike books that were simply scanned into images of individual pages that were difficult to read on small screens. His well-chosen ebooks had an international audience. He developed a collection of English language translations of books by Chinese authors.

As an English major, he also had written several collections of short stories and full-length novels.

There was a copyright dispute (copyright laws were different in different countries) and one of his publisher partners had financial troubles. So, he decided to rebuild his business and move his catalog to other platforms. At the time, it was difficult to move an entire catalog onto four very different platforms, that probably should be called the big four: Amazon, Apple, Barnes & Noble, and Kobo. There were different standards for the metadata about each book; the format of the manuscript (Amazon used Mobi, everyone else used ePub); the size, the file format and resolution of book covers; how banking data was handled; how one selected international markets to publish in; and so on.

A large amount of ebooks are self-published. This has led to some terminology specific to the ebook industry: publisher, seller, and author. The terms discussed below are the most commonly used, but unofficial, standards.

Many self-published authors use the term "publisher" if they have an imprint they wish to have as standard for themselves. This may be "AfterMath" if they are published by either myself or one of the small stable of authors that I arrange to publish.

The term "seller" means just that. It means the person, persons, or organization that actually is able to eventually receive revenues from sales, after a process that I'll describe below.

The term "author" is used in the standard sense.

Many ebook purveyors use all three of the above terms in their metadata descriptions of book. All the big four have the capability to search their catalogs by author name or and by title. Some of them allow searching by publisher or seller.

My son was able to put a large portion of his array of books onto these four publishing platforms. He decided to use what are known as aggregators for much of the rest of his collection of books. An aggregator takes a manuscript in some format, usually Word, but perhaps ePub, standard metadata, a cover, and so on, places all the books in as many outlets as a publisher may desire. In addition, an aggregator can place ebooks in several international stores, and in libraries, with automatic charges for each reader of an ebook.

How do aggregators make their money? Their usual fee is to take 10% of the sales of each ebook. The tradeoff is getting an easier path to publication, wider distribution, and on occasion, print sales, against a lower amount of royalties for each sale to the publisher/seller/author.

Before I corresponded with any of the big four platform providers, I studied their catalogs against one very large spreadsheet I found in my son"s computer. Before I started my analysis, I made a copy of the spreadsheet and used it for all annotations. That way I could be certain to have the original data files taken from my son's computer with no changes, protecting against any later claims.

Using this spreadsheet I checked for each of the many hundreds of titles against the big four platform providers to see which catalog carried which book. This exactly the type of searching that a desktop with a large monitor and a high capacity disk is useful to have.

Here's how I did it. I had four windows open, each one was used to display the catalog of one of the big four, a fifth window for the spread sheet copy.

What did I find? Some of the catalog listings for books listed the seller or the publisher or both. Using that information, I could see some books with each of the two three imprints my son had used long before, dating back to the days when he sold print books. One of the big four's catalog allowed searches for the seller or the publisher, which was useful in finding books in the catalog that were not included in the spreadsheet I was using.

Then I hit pay dirt. Several of the books in on catalog were sold by StreetLib. I recognized the name from an old email my son sent me saying that he was back in the print business. (You have seen this name many times before in this book.

StreetLib was an aggregator! It was based in Italy, but had an office in New York. I called the lawyer who was helping with the estate and she asked a paralegal to contact the company. Out of that effort, I got the following: a new account at StreetLib with a login and password that provided a view of the catalog, monthly statements, tax information, back payments and a simple mechanism for future payments. Ever since the account was set up, I would receive an email late in each month that informed me that an invoice was ready and provided me with a link to their website. I would go to the website and click on the page with the latest invoice available, then click approve button on that invoice. After one or two days, the money would appear in the estate bank account. Both the invoice and the funds were in US dollars.

StreetLib is an Italian company, so it required an invoice before payment, as is typical in Europe, unlike the processes of the big four platforms which either paid monthly, or after a minimum threshold for payments was reached. Fortunately, StreetLib had a US office, so it could arrange simple transfers of funds.

The process is simple.I would get a monthly email, near the end of the month. I would click on a link in the email and get to a website where I could log into the StreetLib account. (I could go to that website directly if I hadn't received the email by the usual time.) I would click on a page with all the invoices and click on the most recent completed one. The money would show up in the estate bank account within two or three days.

There was more pay dirt. I saw a few references to immateriel.fr[1], which was a French company that clearly was also an aggregator. I asked the lawyer's paralegal to do the same thing as she had done for StreetLib. She did so, and

---

1. http://immateriel.fr

then set up the same type of account. Being a French company with no offices in the Uniter States, it had different procedures.

The website was in French, but I could get around using Google Translate on the page and on selected words, if necessary. I also called on my poorly remembered high school French. I could see the amount of sales and I could copy that data.

The company still required invoices, but used PayPal for its payments.I eventually set up a business account with PayPal that I kept separate from my personal use. I searched for the term "Immateriel" in the documents that were stored in files that had been on my son's computer and found a number of documents that apparently had been written to follow a relatively standard template.

I made a copy of one of these files and renamed it "Immateriel Format." I stored this file in a newly created folder with the name "Immateriel." My son evidently tried to simplify the invoicing process and submitted requests for several months at a time. There were naming conventions he used for invoices, like 2020a, 2020b, etc.

I set up a new folder for each year, 2020, 2021, 2022, 2023, etc. Since no invoices were submitted for 2020, I just copied the document with the copy of the invoice format, entered the data that I had found from the website for the appropriate period, edited it, reread it twice, saved it under the name 2020k, converted it to PDF and submitted it via email. Soon the money came in via PayPal.

The next invoice I submitted was in 2021. I did several months at a time using the same process: copy the invoice format to the 2021 folder, renamed the template 2021a, copied the data I needed, edited it to match, reread it twice, converted it to PDF, and emailed it.

I learned to submit for several months at a time, keeping accurate records, and making sure to have an invoice cover only months in the same year. The second invoice in 2021 was labeled 2021b, the next invoice was 2021c, and so on.

These two efforts were successes, but it was clear that I couldn't ask the paralegal I had worked with to do this again, because she was getting ready to relocate from the legal office where she worked. So I ignored seeking out an aggregator Canadian company named Osmora for quite a while in order to find some time to handle other, more pressing, estate issues.

Osmora seemed to be very small and I assumed that I could handle the logistics of payment for this aggregator company myself. They seemed to have another business effort in the same physical location. Unfortunately, I had waited too long to contact this company! When I did contact them, I was informed that they had closed that business and that they had emailed all their clients, informing them of a planned transition to another Canadian company, this one named Gamas. Since there had been no reply from my deceased son's email address, Osmora moved all his books to Gamas, yet another aggregator.

I contacted Gamas and they did have the catalog that Osmora had, which contained only a few books. However, their business model was not the one that was used by StreetLib and Immateriel.fr. Gamas did not take 10% of royalties, as most aggregators did but charged each publisher/seller/author a fixed amount per book as an overhead cost. The amount of royalties paid was so small that they simply sent me a check with no need for me to to provide any of the usual information about me being the Administrator of an estate.

I contacted the aforementioned Kobo directly, using contact information provided by Shelly Adina on her blog. There were lots of delays due to the age of the original agreement between Kobo and my son, and several reorganizations of Kobo's business processes because that Canadian company became a subsidiary of the Japanese conglomerate, Rakuten, so it took a bit of time and several iterations of bureaucratic complexity, but the problem got solved with all back royalties paid and all new royalties paid as they arrived. Many thanks to the Kobo staff and the insights provided by Shelly Adina.

Now I believed that I was ready to contact the remaining three members of the big four that I had not reached out to, Amazon, Apple, and Barnes & Noble. It was clear that these would be tougher. Unfortunately, I ran into difficulties for a variety of reasons.

All these companies have policies in place for treating the books sales made by an author upon the author's death. The personnel involved with bereavement cases will close the accounts of a deceased author, and, after receiving the necessary documentation (death certificate, will or creation of an estate, letter of administration, and similar), will set up a new account and, in some cases, move the author's catalog of books into a new account with the executor or estate Administrator or heir in charge.

The situation is very different for a deceased person who was acting in one or both of the roles of a publisher or seller as defined above. The companies may not provide any information quoting privacy laws. You may be forced to get a writ from a court in the state where the company has its headquarters, Washington, DC for Amazon, California for Apple, and New York for Barnes & Noble. The privacy laws are different in each state and of course for each company.

I contacted Apple by phone, asking for speak to someone about their bereavement process. (I had read some material on this topic from them before I called.) I explained what my role was and what I wanted to do. I explained what documents I had and the person said that I could send an email package containing the documents he wanted and a letter whose content described what I had explained that I wanted. Since I first contacted Apple, I have waited more than a year for a response from them to be recommended to apply for such a writ. Of course, I certainly could have hired a California lawyer but I needed to be able to use the precise language that the writ would have to use in order to have a California court approve it. No response yet.

As a side issue, I had requested Google to provide access to an old, unused email address with them. My goal was to discover any hitherto business arrangements that may have led to obtaining additional revenue to my son's estate. After a long wait, I received an email indicating that Google would be able to respond favorably to a writ for access approved by a California court. My informal cost-benefit analysis suggested that even if filing such a writ was successful, it would not have been worth the effort in terms of time and money.

I had both the same and a different type of problem with Barnes & Noble. As a publisher, seller AND, author, I had my own publishing arrangement with them. I called and got the number of the bereavement area and then I was connected to a person who worked in that office. I explained what my role was and what I wanted to do. Then I explained what documents I had and the person said that I could send an email package containing the documents he wanted and a letter whose content described what I had explained that I wanted. I sent a similar email package to the person I spoke to at Barnes & Noble.

After waiting a reasonable amount of time, I called and I was told that there was nothing in the catalog, in spite of the fact that I seen hundreds of my son's books listed in the Barnes & Noble catalog. Then the person conflated my own personal catalog with Barnes & Noble with my deceased son's. Additional emails and phone calls achieved nothing. I believe this reflects the general reduction in the quality of customer service that occurred after the onset of the Covid pandemic.

I finally decided that I would have to ignore the potential for repayment of three years worth of revenue from royalties for ebooks sold directly through the Apple iBooks and Barnes & Noble platforms, since getting paid seems highly unlikely. Instead, I will move all the books that had been published in these two platforms into the catalog of StreetLib and look for sales there.

In my view, three years of some streams of royalties have been lost to the estate, and there will be a 10% charge on these indirect sales through StreetLib. However, there will be additional revenues for the estate, which is my primary responsibility.

There is one final note about publishing ebooks with Apple and Barnes & Noble. These two platforms allow the same book to be sold with different publisher, seller, and author combinations to be sold. Thus, I do not have to check when I move, say, books from the Barnes & Noble listed as a seller by an old imprint of my son's to be published with the seller being designated as StreetLib. The same is true for the Apple iBooks catalog.

The last of the big four platforms, is Amazon, which is the largest ebook seller. I have not contacted Amazon about moving the titles to the estate, but suspect that there might be difficulties because of the old copyright dispute. It seems better to leave the option of publishing with Amazon alone. Also, Amazon has had strong restrictions against having anyone who publishes with them publish using two or more sellers. Thus a bookseller cannot publish the same book under, say, two different aggregators, or an individual seller and an aggregator, or even two different sellers. It seems best to allow an aggregator to opt to not offer any of these specific books for sale on Amazon, but allow them to be published on every other outlet.

How to Become a Better Decedent and Help Any Future Executors

Everyone will die someday, even you. Here is the minimum set of steps you should take to make sure that you wishes will be carried out by any future executors.

- Choose a person that you wish to be an administrator of your estate.

- Get that person's permission to be your administrator.

- Make a plan for the case of any minor children.

- Choose a person that you trust to be the guardian of any minor children and get their permission to serve.

- Write a proper will and leave a copy with the persons you trust, including any lawyer who helped with this process.

- If the estate is likely to be small, write out the instructions.

- Create a legacy account with Apple, Amazon, Google and the like in order to provide for people to access their loved one's information access. Inform the persons who you wish to designate as legacy contact and make sure they agree before before making the designation official. Keep in mind that policies about whether companies allow legacy contacts or not, and what the legacy contact person may be able to access, may change over time.

- Share passwords, either directly, or via a password manager, that any potential estate administrators can get access to.

- Keep all necessary paper records in a safe place that is known to the potential administrator.

- Provide information on the location of accounts.

Here is an additional step that I am currently taking while preparing for a serious medical procedure. I wrote up a complete description of how all critical payments were made — which bills were paid automatically via credit card, which are paid automatically via bank account transfers, which are paid electronically and which are paid by check, which bills came in via snail mail and which were sent out the same way. I also included which bills required a login to a specific website in order to be paid. Finally, I indicated the times when bills were likely to arrive — monthly, quarterly, yearly, etc.

Tip: Write out detailed instructions about all regular transactions that are handled automatically from, say, a bank account, and all those that require specific actions such as writing checks.

Creating a Digital Legacy

In some ways, creating a digital legacy for a person who left no paper records, only digital ones, might appear to be easy. Part of that was easy, at least in this situation. My deceased son had two computers; one he used for his business together with some of his personal life, and a second computer he used for his fun activities as a karaoke organizer. There are playlists on the karaoke computer that can be created easily and disseminated to some friends and businesses near where he lived. We have already discussed saving the essential nature of the businesses he had earlier in this book.

Photographs that he had on his computers could be curated and organized, and then put together into a family story on some place such as ancestry.com[1] both as part of a nuclear family and as a person in a larger family tree. All the photos his family had of him can be used also. Videos and audios are great if you have them. You can do much of the storage and organization yourself.Note that there are many professional services that can transform audio and video from older analog devices such as audio or video tapes even if the formats used are obsolete and the devices are not available to you.

I think this is more useful than putting photographs on, say, a Facebook page where it may be lost in the weeds. Others may disagree.

You might find it convenient to use a service or software package that is intended for organizational purposes. A CNN report on February 26, 2024 discusses the issues in developing a digital legacy plan at a high level. That report discussed two particular digital legacy planning service companies called Everplans (www.everplans.com[2]) and MyWishes (www.mywishes.co.uk[3]). I have not used either product myself and so cannot recommend them, but they appear to be worth checking out. Note that MyWishes is not based in the US and thus, some differences in privacy laws may come into place.

---

1.   http://ancestry.com

2.   http://www.everplans.com

3.   http://www.mywishes.co.uk

Getting the Death Certificate

At the hight of the Covid epidemic, most cities were essentially locked down and Baltimore was no exception. Getting decent masks to help avoid the virus was extremely difficult. The familiar blue surgical masks were becoming available, but they were intended for blocking bacteria, not the much smaller viruses such as Covid-19.

As was the case with many self-motivated, highly creative people, my son would often stay focused on his writing and not be in touch for weeks at a time. He would only go out to walk his dog or for groceries when absolutely necessary at a time when most restaurants were closed. His mother and I hadn't heard from him for a while and there was no response to text messages or email, which was not unusual. As stated in the Introduction, we found out that he had died when two officers of the Baltimore City Police Department came to our house.

Recall that we had stated earlier that the police had been notified by some of his friends because a delivery of dog food had remained on his front porch steps for a while.

The officers provided us with a card that had the direct number of the Office of the Medical Examiner. It also had the number of a company that specialized in bioremediation and could make the house livable.

The bioremediation company's bill, which had run considerably over $50,000, was paid by the insurance company except for a small deductible amount. All the movable contents of the house were to be removed, for safety reasons.

Here's a listing of the contents of the house: A wallet was saved and given special sterilizing treatment, as were two laptop computers, a cell phone on a Cricket Wireless plan, and a tablet (not an iPad or a Microsoft Surface).

There were no paper records of any sort, so everything financial information I had was in the wallet or electronics. I couldn't get into the electronics without the Death Certificate. I wouldn't go into his wallet until many days had passed and the danger of the virus had disappeared. Paperwork for the utilities, taxes, and similar things were in our names.

In short, there was nothing we had found that would provide adequate identification of the body in order for the Medical Examiner to issue the Death Certificate.

We now describe how the body was finally identified. Unfortunately, his death and the decay caused by the Covid-19 virus meant that the body had decomposed considerably. There were no usable fingerprints because of effects of Covid-19. Recognizing his face would have been impossible, even if anyone would have been allowed into the Medical Examiner's office in order to see his face. His beloved dog died the same night.

As was the case of fingerprints, facial identification was not possible, due to the effects of the virus. There were no visible differences in arm length or leg length.

There were no dental records, because his dentist had retired from his small private practice, was quite old, and could not, or would not, search for records. We did not try medical records due to difficulty getting records during height of Covid. (There had been a broken collar bone at approximately age 13, but providing this knowledge did not provide sufficient information for the Medical Examiner to make an official identification.

Because I was able to describe the specific dental work that was done at age 16— a so-called "Maryland Bridge" that had been installed and provided an anchor on both sides of his bottom of two front teeth to attach an artificial tooth as a replacement for the bottom front tooth that had never grown in as a permanent tooth in detail to the Medical Examiner, he issued the death certificate.

References

Please note that websites may be reorganized or changed at any time.

- Adina, Shelly, https://shelleyadina.com/wp-content/uploads/2016/06/Logins_UponTheDeath.pdf.

- Clifford, Denis, "Plan Your Estate 14 ed.", Berkeley, Ca., 2018.

- Pierce, Margaret E., "The Complete Guide to Wills, Trusts & Estates," Atlantic Pub. Group, Ocala, Florida, 2008.

- Tompor, Susan, ""Requesting a tax return will cost you. Here's how to get it for free., Detroit Free Press, March 12, 224. (Reprinted in USA Today on line.)"

- Recovering crypto, general information: https://cryptoassetrecovery.com/posts/i-had-a-death-in-my-family-how-do-i-recover-their-crypto.

- Recovering bitcoin, general information: https://bitcoin.stackexchange.com/questions/18663/recovering-bitcoins-after-the-owners-death.

- Coinbase policy general information: https://help.coinbase.com/en/coinbase/managing-my-account/other/how-do-i-gain-access-to-a-deceased-family-members-coinbase-account

- www.unclaimed.org[1]

- www.MissingMoney.com[2]

- www.treasurtdirect.gov/indiv/indiv.htm[3]

---

1. http://www.unclaimed.org

2. http://www.MissingMoney.com

3. http://www.treasurtdirect.gov/indiv/indiv.htm

- www.treasurydirect.gov/email.htm[4]

- www.treasurydurect.gov/TH/THGateway[5].

- LifeWire, Finding Where Apple Mail Stores Mail Messages, www.LifeWire.com/find-and-open-stored-attachments-1172808[6]

- Facebook bereavement information: www.facebook.com/help/275013292838654/?helpref=hc_fnav[7]

- X bereavement information: https://help.twitter.com/en/rules-and-policies/contact-x-about-a-deceased-family-members-account.

- TikTok general help website: https://support.tiktok.com/en.

- LinkedIn bereavement information: https://www.linkedin.com/help/linkedin/answer/a1336663.

- YouTube bereavement information (YouTube is a subsidiary of Google):   https://support.google.com/accounts/troubleshooter/6357590?hl=en.

---

4. http://www.treasurydirect.gov/email.htm

5. http://www.treasurydurect.gov/TH/THGateway

6. http://www.LifeWire.com/find-and-open-stored-attachments-1172808

7. http://www.facebook.com/help/275013292838654/?helpref=hc_fnav

Checklists

A version of each of these checklists is available in Excel format for free download at either of the two indicated directories on the chosen websites www.rleach.com/spreadsheets/estate/[1] or www.distance-college.com/spreadsheets/estate/[2]

For the deceased person's estate checklist, select either of the files available on either (www.rleach.com/spreadsheets/estate/Estate.xlsx[3] or www.distance-college.com/spreadsheets/estate/Estate.xlsx[4]

- Get at least ten copies of the death certificate.

- Check for a will in safe deposit box, inside home or with lawyer.

- Save all papers, until you have read them at least twice.

- Contact the deceased person's friends and family.

- Check safe deposit boxes.

- Locate Social Security Number.

- Get a lawyer to help set up the estate.

- Ask to set up a "small estate" if the known values of the estate allow it. This avoids probate.

- Get an EIN

- Create new email address just for estate business.

---

1. http://www.rleach.com/spreadsheets/estate

2. http://www.distance-college.com/spreadsheets/estate

3. http://www.rleach.com/spreadsheets/estate/Estate.xlsx

4. http://www.distance-college.com/spredsheets/estate/estate.xlsx

• Find a place in your home to keep records in a safe place.

• Keep all estate records.

• Search bank accounts.

• Search for custodial accounts, and 529-type plans.

• Get at least one year of bank statements.

• Talk to credit card providers.

• Get at least one year of credit card statements.

• Call or write all possible brokerage firms to see if the deceased had an account there.

• Call or write Treasury Direct.

• Search MissingMoney.com[5] and unclaimed.org[6] for each state in which the deceased was known to have lived. Continue to do this, because new properties may be added at any time.

• File estate tax returns in a timely manner.

• Distribute estate income in sufficient amounts to avoid the estate paying income tax. Make sure that estate payouts exceed estate income.

• Search email messages sent to or from the deceased to your computer or smartphone.

• Access data stored on computers, getting technical help if necessary.

---

5. http://MissingMoney.com

6. http://unclaimed.org

• Access data stored on smartphones and tablets, getting technical help if necessary.

• Check for a legacy contact successor on Apple.

• Check for a legacy contact successor on Amazon.

• Check for a legacy contact successor on Google.

• If you need a writ to get access to information considered private by a tech company such as Google or apple, use a California-based lawyer.

• Pay for cloud service, if possible, while waiting to get digital access.

• Understand the deceased person's business.

• Search electronic wallets.

• Search for peer-to-peer transactions.

• Search cryptocurrency wallets, if applicable.

• Reconstruct the deceased person's business, if possible.

• Examine the deceased person's known personal and business websites.

• Use the Wayback machine at https://web.archive.org.

• Use social media, as applicable.

• Manage the estate, paying all legal fees, bequests, and taxes.

• Have a successor plan for yourself in your role as estate Administrator.

• Create a digital legacy for the deceased person.

Use either of the links below to provide an Excel spreadsheet that can help you to prepare for your own estate.
   www.rleach.com/spreadsheets/estate/PrepareYourEstate.xlsx[7]
   or, as an alternative location,
   www.distance-college.com/spreadsheets/estate/PrepareYourEstate.xlsx[8]

- Organize records.

- Create a will.

- Organize all paper records.

- Get a safe deposit box, if possible.

- Share phone and computer passwords, if feasible.

- Save all passwords on a password manager, either the one built in or a commercial one.

- Set up a legacy contact successor on Apple

- Set up a legacy contact successor on Amazon

- Set up a legacy contact successor on Google.

- Start planning a digital legacy for yourself and family.

---

7.   http://www.rleach.com/spreadsheets/estate/PrepareYourEstate.xlsx

8.   http://www.distance-college.com/spreadsheets/estate/PrepareYourEstate.xlsx

Also by Ronald J. Leach

Software Reuse: Methods, Models, Costs, Second Edition
Why 2K?
Where Have All The Templates Gone?
User Guide to Microfilm and Microfiche
The 101 Most Important UNIX and Linux Commands
Baltimore Blue and Freddie Gray
Digitizing Microfilm and Microfiche
Managing an Estate Without Paper Records

About the Author

About the Author

I recently retired from being a professor of computer science at **Howard University** for over 25 years, with 9 of those years as a department chair. (I was a math professor for 16 years before that.) While I was department chair, we sent more students to work at Microsoft in the 2004-5 academic year than any other college or university in the United States. We also established a graduate certificate program in computer security, which became the largest certificate program at the university. I had major responsibility for working with technical personnel to keep our department's hundreds of computers functional and virus-free, while providing email service to several hundred users. We had to withstand constant hacker attacks and we learned how to reduce the vulnerability of our computer systems.

As a scholar/researcher, I studied complex computer systems and their behavior when attacked or faced with heavy, unexpected loads. I wrote five books on computing, from particular programming languages, to the internal structure of sophisticated operating systems, to the development and efficient creation of highly complex applications. My long-term experience with computers (I had my first computer programming course in 1964) has helped me understand the nature of many of the computer attacks by potential identity thieves and, I hope, be able to explain them and how to defend against them, to a general audience of non-specialists. More than 5,000 people have attended my lectures on identity theft; many others have seen them on closed-circuit television.

I have written more than twenty books, and more than 120 technical articles, most of which are in technical areas.

My interests in data storage and access meshed well with my genealogical interests when I wrote the Genealogy Technology column of the **Maryland Genealogical Society Journal** for several years. I was the editor or co-editor of that society's journal for many years.

About the Publisher

AfterMath is a small, highly selective publisher based in Baltimore, Maryland, focusing on high-quality technical books and selected thoughtfully written fiction.